Rational Expectations

Rational Expectations

An Elementary Exposition

G.K. Shaw

St. Martin's Press   New York

© G.K. Shaw, 1984

ISBN 0-312-66402-8
ISBN 0-312-66403-6 (pbk.)

Library of Congress Cataloging in Publication Data

Shaw, G.K. (Graham Keith), 1938–
    Rational expectations.

    Bibliography: p.
    Includes index.
    1. Rational expectations (Economic theory) I. Title.
HB172.5.S5224   1984   339'.0724   83-19252
ISBN 0-312-66402-8
ISBN 0-312-66403-6 (pbk.)

To the memory of E.C. Wynne-Edwards

rational expectations... is an offshoot of Chicago-monetarism... the radical wing of monetarism. It is best known for the startling policy conclusions... to wit, that macro-economic policies, both monetary and fiscal, are ineffective, *even in the short run*... it is the extreme antithesis of orthodox Keynesianism... it contradicts... the Austrian Theory of money and the business cycle (of Hayek and Mises) which asserts a basic *unneutrality* of money and it goes beyond Friedman's monetarism which... does not exclude quick though transitory effects on output and employment...

Gottfried Haberler

Contents

Preface

Whatever charges are levied against the present volume originality will not be one of them. The book is unashamedly eclectic and its purpose entirely pedagogical. It reflects the author's sincerely held belief that if there is anything worth saying in economics then it should be possible to make it intelligible to first year students who have but a basic grounding in economic theory. It is conceded that there are dangers in this philosophy, not least that it precipitates the charge of superficiality, lack of rigour and, on occasion, possible distortion of the true position of the participants in the debate. Nonetheless, the position taken here is that these risks are worth running especially if the outcome of the endeavour is to provoke the better student to pursue the subject at a more ambitious level. To this end, a relatively comprehensive bibliography is appended.

I am indebted to my colleagues David Greenaway and Professor Alan Peacock for many insights and the eradication of errors and also to Rob Grant for providing valuable source material. The rational expectation that this project would be speedily and efficiently abetted by the cheerful secretarial assistance of Linda Waterman proved entirely correct. Finally, I would like to express my thanks to Edward Elgar, of Wheatsheaf Books, for first suggesting the venture.

G.K. Shaw
May 1983

1 An Illustration

Let us assume, by some great flight of the imagination, the existence of a country possessed of a zero rate of inflation. Further, let us suppose that within this idyllic setting a certain Mr Well-to-Do is willing to grant credit in return for a 5 per cent reward on his outlay, whilst equally, a Mr Need-a-Loan is willing to pay 5 per cent interest in order to obtain a supply of credit. It is reasonable to assume that they will come together and negotiate a contractual agreement, let us say for one year, at the interest rate of 5 per cent. Let us suppose that the experience of Mr Well-to-Do and Mr Need-a-Loan is generalised to the entire economy so that the market economy reconciles the conflicting objectives of creditors and debtors with a market clearing rate of interest of 5 per cent. Here, with a zero inflation rate, nominal and real interest rates are equated.[1] This situation we depict with the aid of Figure 1.1.

Utopian settings, as the story of Adam and Eve reminds us, seldom persist for long. The dictum that if something can go wrong it will is too often proved correct. Let us suppose that the fly in the ointment takes the shape of an ambitious Minister of Finance. Believing that investment and hence economic growth will be stimulated by a reduction in real interest rates the Minister decides to utilise the banking sector to expand the supply of credit. Accordingly, he announces his intention of increasing the money supply, let us say at the rate of 10 per cent annually, in the reasonable belief (at least to judge from orthodox elementary textbooks) that interest rates will fall in consequence.

However, let us suppose that Mr Well-to-Do, being a well informed citizen, notices the Minister's announcement.

1

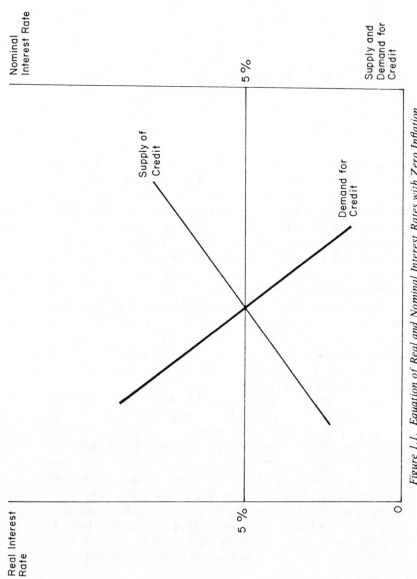

Figure 1.1. Equation of Real and Nominal Interest Rates with Zero Inflation

Moreover, being of a somewhat gullible nature, let us suppose he believes it. Finally, let us assume that he once attended an introductory economics course and encountered a famous equation of exchange in the form

$$MV = PQ = Y^n$$

where M denotes the money stock, V its velocity of circulation, Q is the level of output and P its aggregate price level so that PQ is identically equal to nominal GNP or Y^n. If he assumes that V and Q will remain constant he will instantly conclude that the effect of increasing the money supply by some 10 per cent annually will be to generate an equal annual increase in the inflation rate; $\Delta M = \Delta P$. He will conclude, not unreasonably, that if he is to maintain a 5 per cent real return upon his outlay, he will require a nominal rate of interest of 15 per cent.

Suppose now that Mr Need-a-Loan is equally well informed, equally gullible and also attended the same introductory economics course. He too anticipates a future yearly inflation rate of 10 per cent. Let us also assume that the experience of our two central characters is generalised to the entire economy; all creditors and debtors have become reconciled to a future 10 per cent rate of inflation. What are the consequences? It is reasonable to assume that all creditors will demand a 15 per cent nominal interest return and all debtors will be willing to concede it since both sides of the market will be motivated by *real* as opposed to nominal values.

Let us now stretch our flight of imagination to the limit and assume that the Minister of Finance actually does what he said he would—that is, he brings about a 10 per cent increase in monetary growth. Moreover, let us suppose the economy behaves in accordance with our simple equation of exchange and generates a 10 per cent inflation rate. What has the Minister achieved?

The answer in simple terms is precisely nothing. By anticipating the effects of the Minister's policy and seeking to accommodate it the joint actions of creditors and debtors have effectively negated it. The real rate of interest remains unchanged at 5 per cent per annum and since investment is a function of real interest rates there will be no positive change in investment spending and consequently no positive impact upon the rate of economic growth. All that the Minister has achieved is a change in nominal values by transforming a zero inflation rate into a 10 per cent inflation rate with all the inconveniences and costs that that implies. His policy measure to stimulate the economy has been rendered impotent. Disillusioned with elementary economic textbooks the Minister resigns and seeks a career in merchant banking.

The above parable is admittedly *simpliste* and as the reader will readily appreciate written very much tongue in cheek. Nonetheless, it does serve to bring out some aspects of the rational expectations thesis and controversy. First of all, it is based upon the assumption that all economic agents (in the present case all our debtors and creditors) formulate their expectations rationally. That is to say, they formulate their expectations not solely upon the basis of what they have observed in the past but also in the light of all current information and knowledge *including the policy statements of the Minister of Finance.* Moreover, they utilise this information in the most efficient way possible. That is to say, they incorporate this information into a model of the economy which they believe accurately describes the way in which the economy actually operates. In so doing, they generate a prediction—in fact a mathematical expectation—of the future course of inflation. Using this estimation of the expected inflation rate they modify their behaviour in such a manner as to negate the intentions of the macro policy authorities should the economy respond as they believe it will. This simplified example illustrates the stark and in many respects disturbing conclusion of the rational expectations hypothesis, namely that the governing authorities are unable to pursue effective macro-economic stabilisation policies. Their ability to influence *real* variables, such as output, employment, real wages and real interest rates, is seriously called into question. There is no question of the authorities' ability to influence nominal values by changing the rate of monetary growth; what is questioned is the ability of the authorities to exercise any influence whatsoever upon real magnitudes as conventionally implied in Keynesian demand management strategies. In effect, we are back in a classical world postulating a dichotomy between the real and monetary sectors with the government virtually powerless to influence the real side of the economy which, determined by natural forces, will eventually seek its 'natural' level. Moreover, it must be emphasised that this conclusion of the rational expectations hypothesis is not merely an assertion of the invariability of real values from their *long-term* natural level; what is asserted is that no departure of real values is permitted from their natural levels *even in the short term*. As our parable fully illustrates, our unfortunate Minister of Finance never even gets a token run for his money. In the conclusions of the rational expectations doctrine, there is no question of any trade-off between short-term influence on real values offset by longer-term inflationary consequences—a trade-off which Keynesian oriented economists have been increasingly willing to concede in the face of monetarist critique. Indeed, one way to paraphrase the rational expectations thesis would be to say that it abolishes the distinction between the short run and the long run. Values are maintained at their equilibrium level—at the market clearing prices—at all points in time. Implicit in this statement, of course, is an assumption to the effect that there exists almost unlimited flexibility in the adjustment of nominal values.

Implicit in our simple illustration are, of course, the conditions under which these stark and foreboding conclusions of rational expectations need not apply. Suppose, for example, that having concluded a 15 per cent nominal interest rate agreement in anticipation of a 10 per cent inflation rate, our creditors and debtors suddenly found themselves confronted by an unscrupulous Minister of Finance increasing monetary growth by 20 per cent and thereby generating 20 per cent inflation. Then, until such time as the agreements could be renegotiated, the real rate of interest would be negative with possibly very beneficial effects upon overall growth rates. Thus, the ability of economic agents correctly to anticipate the intentions of the authorities, or alternatively the ability of the authorities to mislead and befuddle economic agents as to their future intentions becomes of critical importance to the effective scope of interventionist macro-economic policy. This aspect of the rational expectations thesis carries, if only implicitly, one very important side effect. The more government economic policy actually seems sensible—that is, the more it is seen to be countercyclical in character—the more readily will it be anticipated by sensible maximum welfare seeking economic agents. In contrast, the more absurd, capricious or even arbitrary is government policy seen to be, the more effective will be its influence upon real magnitudes. For the Keynesian trained economist this is indeed a daunting conclusion. Demand management through a system of generating *randomised autonomous shocks* to the system is hardly likely to be conducive to the attainment of targetted values of output and employment. Certainly, it is a far cry from the ideal of 'fine tuning' characteristic of the earlier Keynesian optimism.

Secondly, our simple illustration rests upon the supposition that Mr Well-to-Do and Mr Need-a-Loan both think and deal in real terms and are never misled by movements solely in nominal values. The extent to which this is true is, of course, an empirical question, but it seems reasonable to posit that the following behaviour pattern might hold. When we move from a situation of zero inflation, or alternatively from a very low rate of inflation to a relatively rapid rate of inflation in a reasonably short time, some money illusion will be likely to persist. Time will be required to adjust to the painful experience of higher inflation rates and during this period real interest might decline. This situation would not exist indefinitely since creditors would ultimately adjust to the fact that their real interest returns were declining, but during this interim or transitional period there might be some scope for a real influence upon growth variables. In contrast, when high rates of inflation have prevailed for long periods, economic agents will be all too aware of the drawbacks of money illusion and will most certainly be conditioned to think in real terms. This is all too well borne out by the recent inflationary experience in the United Kingdom and the United States where trade union negotiators have displayed an increasing degree of sophistication in their approach to wage bargaining. Not only are wage contracts drawn up with respect to anticipated future inflation rates but on occasions the agreement is effectively index linked, which safeguards against the possibility of the future inflation rate being underestimated. This argument would suggest, then, that the degree to which the macro authorities might be able to influence the economy would not be symmetrical over the phases of the trade cycle and would tend to be greater in periods of relatively low inflation and *vice versa*.

Thirdly, no matter whether our economic agents are free from money illusion or not, they may to all intents and purposes be locked into a binding agreement which cannot be altered in the short term. Suppose, for example, that in our simple illustration the initial contracts were drawn up for a five-year period during which the obligation on both parties was binding. Then, our Minister of Finance would have enjoyed a four-year period during which his policies might be seen to be working precisely as intended. Such a time span, it may be noted, would in all probability be sufficient to carry him through the next electoral test and also possibly to promotion to higher office. The pessimistic policy conclusions of the rational expectations thesis, therefore, depend critically upon the degree of price flexibility prevailing in various markets. Needless to say, if economic agents found themselves disadvantaged in this way, they would have the incentive to progressively shorten the period of obligation implied in any formal contract. Nonetheless, there are costs in so doing, not least the cost of uncertainty. To sign a wage contract, for example, to last for a one-year, two-year or three-year period, is to guarantee a certain income stream over that period. It is a form of insurance which could be jeopardised by a weekly contract. Clearly, in any given inflationary setting there would exist some optimal contractual period to be determined by the agents to the contract. The question which then becomes crucial for the scope of interventionist macro-policy, is whether this contractual period is sufficient to allow the government to change tack and affect real variables during the period of the contract.

Several other important reservations could be made to modify the moral of our simple fable. Mr Well-to-Do may possess a different model of the economy from that possessed by Mr Need-a-Loan. He might be excused, for example, for thinking (had he attended a more Keynesian oriented introductory economics course) that a 10 per cent increase in monetary growth might be offset, wholly or in part, by a reduction in the velocity of circulation of money so that the expected impact upon prices was less than the eventual 10 per cent. Again, both parties to the contract might have a different view of how the economy behaves from the way it behaves in fact. They may lack crucial information and data which would give them a better idea of the actual movements of the economy, and this information may be difficult or expensive to obtain.

These reservations and qualifications, *inter alia*, will be developed in greater detail in the following pages. In so doing, we will demonstrate that the real world is a far cry from the imaginary world of our parable. Before turning to these and related issues, however, we will begin by examining the need to deal with expectations if economic theory is going to be usefully applied. We will then examine alternative ways in which expectations have been incorporated into economic theory in the past, paying particular attention to the static expectations thesis, to Keynes and expectations, and to the doctrine of adaptive expectations. We will attempt to show that the rational expectations thesis is a logical outcome of the sense of dissatisfaction which these statements have generated in the past, especially in the context of inflationary conditions. We will also argue that the rational expectations hypothesis is intimately linked with both monetarism and supply side economics and is very much in keeping with the recent emphasis upon the subordination of fiscal policy to monetary policy which has occurred in both the United Kingdom and the United States. Finally, we will undertake a critical review of the policy implications and pitfalls of the rational expectations thesis; we will not, however, attempt more than a cursory mention of the current controversy concerning the empirical evidence. A detailed assessment of the evidence and of the difficulties in the interpretation of it would take us far beyond the confines of the present volume both in terms of length and level of exposition.

NOTE

1   When inflation rates are positive it is necessary to subtract the inflation rate from the nominal rate of interest in order to obtain the real rate of interest.

2 The Need for Expectations Theory

Virtually all economic decisions, other than the trivial, involve time. The most obvious example concerns the decision to invest when outlays are incurred in the current period in order to generate future income streams to be realised over the life of the asset. In the case of a project such as the Channel Tunnel, for example, the asset life may be considerable and even if the most distant returns are virtually entirely discounted the time profile of the pay-off period will run into several years. Clearly, in such an undertaking, any sensible decision must involve making an estimation of future demand patterns, energy prices and the costs of alternative means of transport. Such estimates may be based upon the extrapolation of past trends or, alternatively, may be based upon different scenarios involving optimistic or pessimistic assumptions and generating a range of possible outcomes with differing probabilities applied to each. In either case, the investment decision is based upon a set of expectations concerning future costs, prices and markets. We will examine the uncertainty surrounding the investment act in more detail below; for the moment we will indicate other choice situations where a sensible or welfare maximising decision cannot be undertaken without some estimate of the conditions expected to pertain in the future.

Consider the theory of consumer behaviour, for example. A decision to save implies the decision to postpone consumption until some future time. Thus, in deciding whether or not to save or in deciding upon how much to save in any given period one would need to consider the future rate of inflation in relation to

9

current interest rate yields. Realistically, one would also be influenced by one's expectation of future income as the permanent income hypothesis of consumption behaviour and similar statements make abundantly clear. Elementary text-book expositions of inter-temporal choice frequently adopt the simplifying assumption of a two-period analysis in which the incomes pertaining to each period are known with absolute certainty. It is then a comparatively simple matter, given conventional indifference curve analysis, to determine the optimal combination between consumption and saving. In practice, however, the time horizon with which individual consumers have to concern themselves will extend well beyond the immediate future and expectations of distant income streams will be held with a considerable degree of uncertainty. The greater the degree of uncertainty the greater the standard deviation pertaining to the mean value of the anticipated future income stream. Both factors, the mean value of the probability distribution and its dispersion, will logically enter into the consumption decision of the rational individual. This is not to assert that all individuals will respond in the same manner to a given expectation; their response will differ according to their propensity towards risk aversion. What is being asserted is simply that the analysis of consumer behaviour will be incomplete unless it incorporates some measure of expectations formation. Equally, expectations enter into decisions to purchase durable consumption goods whose existing prices may reflect heavy initial development costs; likewise expectations of tax rate changes will often influence consumption patterns, as frequently witnessed in last minute attempts to beat the budget.

Similar considerations apply to shorter-term portfolio investments, to dealings in commodity markets and especially in forward foreign exchange markets. The participants' behaviour is conditioned by the existence of uncertainty and by the expectations they must form, in the light of this uncertainty, concerning future events and in particular future prices. Economic theory, if it is to be convincing, must contain some means of modelling expectations and taking into account how changes in the prevailing state of expectation may feed back upon the pattern of economic behaviour. Unfortunately, to date, expectations have not, generally speaking, been dealt with in a manner commensurate with their importance. Indeed, by far the vast majority of economic models do not deal with expectations at all or, if this is perhaps an overstatement, they deal with them only implicitly by assuming that they are in some way already incorporated into parameter values. Consider, for example, the elementary theory of the supply of labour. It is usual to assert that the supply of labour will be a function of the real wage so that

$$N = N\left(\frac{W}{P}\right)$$

where N is the amount of labour hours, W the nominal wage and P the general price index. Moreover, it is conventional to assume that the function is positive so that an increase in the real wage will generate an increase in labour supply. This assertion in itself, however, does not specify the quantity of labour which will be supplied at any given wage rate. In Figure 2.1, for example, the information given above would be consistent with any one of the indicated supply curves. How do we select among them?

It would seem reasonable to assume that the amount of labour that will be offered at any given wage will be conditioned by what labour had been accustomed to receiving in the past. Suppose that at the wage $\bar{W}/P$ the quantity of labour $\bar{Q}$ had been offered and taken up as indicated by the supply curve N^1. When labour becomes unemployed it will, initially at least, continue to expect to find employment at the wage $\bar{W}/P$. As the period of unemployment extends and this expectation proves unfounded the reservation wage will be lowered. The supply curve gradually shifts downwards towards N^2 and subsequently N^3. This type of behaviour is, of course, applicable to search theories of unemployment. All that we wish to emphasise here is that when drawing a supply curve to summarise the information contained in the above equation, the *position* of the curve implicitly reflects a state of expectation upon the part of labour.

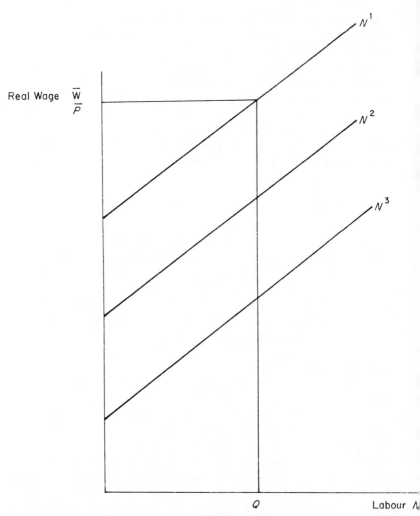

Figure 2.1. *Labour Supply Curves Consistent with* $N = N(W/P)$

THE PRESENT VALUE OF AN ASSET

To reinforce the need for some form of expectations theory in modelling economic decision-taking let us consider again the act of investment. What is required is some means of determining how much it is worthwhile to pay in order to acquire a durable capital asset which yields a saleable product. What is involved in determining its present value?

Over the life of the asset, say n years, the asset will produce an output Q, selling at a price P. It will also involve user costs U, consisting of materials cost, labour cost, fuel and so forth. The net proceeds in each year ($PQ - U$) will in all probability be subject to some form of taxation at rate t. At the end of its useful life the asset in question may possess a scrap value J. Assuming it is possible to determine these magnitudes with some reasonable degree of accuracy it is then necessary to discount the net income streams by the appropriate interest rate to determine the present value V—i.e., what it is worth paying in order to acquire the asset.[1] Accordingly,

$$V = \frac{(P_1 Q_1 - U_1)(1 - t_1)}{(1 + i)^1} + \frac{(P_2 Q_2 - U_2)(1 - t_2)}{(1 + i)^2} + \cdots$$

$$\frac{(P_n Q_n - U_n)(1 - t_n)}{(1 + i)^n} + \frac{J_n(1 - t_n)}{(1 + i)^n}$$

Hence, a rational attempt to evaluate the present value of the asset will require making some judgement about the following unknown factors:

1　The life of the asset n. In all probability this will be known with a good deal of uncertainty since it will depend upon how quickly it is made obsolescent by the pace of technical change and innovation. In certain industries the pace of technical change may be substantial and the more distant income streams will tend to be discounted accordingly.

2　The potential scrap value J. For exactly the same reasons as mentioned above the value of J will be decidedly uncertain.

3　The annual output Q. Whilst the productive potential of the asset will be known within very small limits the actual output may depend upon the general state of the business cycle and accordingly uncertainty will surround the most distant output estimates.

4   The price of the product P. Similar reasoning will imply uncertainty as to the price which may be expected in subsequent years.

5   The user cost U. Again this will be uncertain, being dependent upon wage negotiations, unforeseen factors such as OPEC decisions and the like. Again the more distant the user cost the greater the degree of uncertainty, but it is likely that changes in U will mirror changes in P.

6   The rate of taxation t. Again this will be virtually unknowable beyond the immediate income periods being essentially subject to political decisions.

7   The interest rate i. Once again the interest rate may be foreseen with some certainty for the initial periods but beyond that its value may be uncertain.

It follows that the accurate determination of the present value of an asset involves making a detailed assessment as to future economic trends and variables. In all probability, risk aversion will dictate that the more distant income streams are discounted entirely. Moreover, it seems reasonable to posit that some of the unknowns will exhibit compensatory changes whilst still others, as, for example, the rate of change in taxation, might reasonably be given a mean expected value of zero. Nonetheless, there will remain a considerable degree of uncertainty which will require making some estimate concerning future factor and product prices to permit a rational investment decision to be made. It follows that if economic theory is going to attempt to formulate an explanation of how the economy does in fact behave, then it must also attempt to explain how such estimates of future prices are to be formed. In short, economic theory must incorporate, if only implicitly, some statement as to expectations behaviour and of the factors that give rise to changes in such expectations.

Few economists would be inclined to deny the above conclusion. Where they might differ would be over the question of how expectations are to be formally treated. The advocates of the rational expectations doctrine are simply arguing that it is the most efficient way to formulate one's expectation of the future and that, accordingly, an individual not using rational expectations will not be pursuing maximising behaviour. If we assume that individual agents do follow maximising strategy then this statement is tantamount to saying that individuals do indeed formulate their expectations rationally, regardless of how economists choose to model them. It follows that if the models do not incorporate rational expectations formation then the predictions of the models may be found wanting.

Now the simple fact of the matter is that most econometric models which are used for macro-forecasting, including comparatively large-scale models, deal with expectations formation in a manner which can only be described as naive and distinctly non-rational. The usual treatment is to make the expected future values of a variable depend solely upon the past behaviour of that variable. Moreover, the relationship between expected and past values is usually presented as static and unchanging. Thus, for example, the future expected price of oil will be based solely upon the extrapolation of past values, completely ignoring the fact that OPEC producers have today announced a major price cut or the government a major tax rise. This failure of econometric forecasting models to relate expectations formation to current conditions and policy announcements is doubtless one reason why such models provide inaccurate forecasts of future economic conditions. However, the failure to incorporate rational expectations specifications within such models is held by rational expectations theorists to be far more serious and in particular to invalidate much macro-economic policy formulation.

In devising the appropriate macro-economic strategy treasury officials will consider how tax, expenditure or monetary changes will impinge upon the economy. For this purpose, they will invoke a theoretical model which they feel accurately describes the functioning of the economy. Normally, the values taken by the parameters of the model will have been estimated by normal statistical techniques including regression analysis. Certain values taken by the coefficients may be held with a certain degree of uncertainty but, nonetheless, within a given range it will be possible to simulate the effects of a given policy change. In recent years, the enormous advance in computer technology and applications has made it a relatively simple exercise for such simulations to be carried out by an interested party at comparatively moderate cost.[2] The results of such simulations allow the Treasury authorities to recommend that particular combination of policy measures which promises to approximate the attainment of declared targets most closely.[3]

However, if expectations are indeed formed rationally then such simulation exercises are invalidated from the outset. For the rational expectations thesis argues that utility maximising individuals will perceive whether macro-economic policy is being expansionary or contractionary, will form expectations of future inflation rates in the light of this perception and will then modify their behaviour pattern in accordance with their revised outlook. Naive forecasting models which assume that economic agents' expectations are but mere extrapolations of former values ignore completely the influence of policy changes and announcements in changing behaviour patterns. Not only are the forecasts of the model incorrect but the entire process of policy formulation is invalidated by the adoption of an incorrect unchanging behavioural response to the policy change. The implications of such a conclusion are indeed of enormous import for all those engaged in modelling and forecasting activity. This damning critique of policy simulation exercises stems from Lucas (1976) and suggests that parameters estimated from previous policies will be entirely inappropriate in the simulation of new policies. The implications of the 'Lucas Critique' are of enormous import for all those engaged in economic modelling and forecasting and unless this difficulty can be accommodated it implies that a considerable investment in econometric model building will have been wasted.

If expectations are not formed rationally, then existing econometric models may possess greater justification even if their forecasts are not always accurate. Whether expectations are or are not formed rationally is thus of enormous importance not only to macro-economic theory but also to policy formulation and control. This is a question to which the present volume will attempt to provide an answer. For the moment, however, we will consider alternative means of expectations formation invoked by economic theory and attempt to assess the realism of the underlying assumptions.

NOTES

1   Since £ 100 to be received in one year's time is worth less than £ 100 to be received next week, and £ 100 to be received in fifty years' time is worth a good deal less. In general, the present value of a future income receipt will be lower the more distant its date of receipt and the higher the rate of interest. More formally, the present value of an income receipt Y, to be received in t years' time is indicated by

$$V = \frac{Y}{(l + i)^t}$$

where i is the market rate of interest. For derivation of the above formula see Greenaway and Shaw (1983), Chapter 3.

2   In the United Kingdom, the 1975 Industry Act expressly makes the Treasury Model available for public use; it has been utilised by private forecasting associations, such as the Economists' Intelligence Unit, the TUC, business and the opposition Labour party, and is indeed available at no charge to any member of parliament. For comment on the models see Holden, Peel and Thompson (1983).

3   Strictly speaking the Treasury recommendation may reflect not just the proximity of the mean expected value of the policy measure to targetted values but also the standard deviation around the mean. Certain policy options may be ruled out because they carry a risk of an 'unacceptable' outcome.

3 Non-Rational Expectations

Rational expectations developed partly as a reaction against alternative specifications of expectations formation which may accordingly be characterised as *non-rational* or *naive* expectations. Amongst the more important of these statements are the static expectations thesis, which has the overriding virtue of simplicity, and the thesis of adaptive expectations, which possesses the merit that it can readily be incorporated into econometric modelling exercises and be subject to empirical test. Adaptive expectations are essentially extrapolative expectations; such expectations are derived as a weighted average of past experience. A common example in economic literature is provided by the permanent income hypothesis of Milton Friedman (1957) in which permanent income is derived from a geometrically declining weighted average of past income levels. We will examine both these statements of expectations formation in the present chapter. In addition, in view of the fact that the policy implications derived from rational expectations theory are so much at variance with Keynesian economics generally, it is instructive to examine how Keynes dealt with the existence of expectations and more importantly with destabilising changes in expectations.

STATIC EXPECTATIONS

The simplest way of modelling expectations in economic theory is to assume that conditions prevailing today will be maintained in all subsequent time periods. Expected future values then become identified with current values. This formulation can be considered on one of two levels. One can postulate that, for example, prices or the level of output in subsequent periods will be identical to prices or output levels prevailing today. Alternatively, and in a more sophisticated guise, the static expectations thesis can be formulated to argue that the expected rate of inflation or the rate of economic growth in future periods will be the same as the rate of inflation or growth rate prevailing today. In either case, the static expectations hypothesis is tantamount to assuming that the economy has achieved a steady state equilibrium.

Much of classical economics tacitly assumed the existence of static expectations. Moreover, the classical economist tended to consider such expectations to be held with a reasonable degree of certainty and not to be subject to sudden and violent fluctuation. Consequently, it was a comparatively simple matter to postulate market clearing situations with the reasonable presumption that the equilibrium so obtained would be maintained indefinitely. In this connection it is interesting to note that Keynes (1937), in his celebrated defence of the *General Theory*, placed great emphasis upon the unstable nature of long-term expectations as signalling a major departure from the classical framework he sought to deny. We will examine Keynes' treatment of expectations later in this chapter. For the moment, we will content ourselves by indicating the strengths and shortcomings of the static expectations thesis.

First of all, the static expectations thesis does possess some initial credibility. If a given price ratio were to prevail for a given period of time, then for many people it would become identified with the 'norm'. Thus, for example, one tends to think in terms of a normal rate of interest or a normal rate of exchange as that rate which has been prevailing in the immediately preceding period. More distant experiences tend to be more heavily discounted and very distant experiences may be ignored entirely in the formation of one's expectations of the future. This is perhaps a simple way of saying that the facts of the current situation exercise a disproportionate influence upon one's expectations of the future. Secondly, in a world of uncertainty (and in a certain world there would be no need for any expectations formation whatsoever) it may well be that the probability distribution concerning possible outcomes is symmetrical around the current value. In this case, the mathematically expected mean valuation of the outcome is coincident with current values. Even if symmetry does not exist, it may well be that the mathematical expectation of a gain or loss upon the current price is zero in the aggregate. Indeed, this is the way in which we would expect an efficient market to operate. The stock market's evaluation of an asset, for example, gives a price which reflects all available evidence and posits that given uncertainty a capital gain or loss is equally likely in the absence of long term trend factors such as expected inflation or economic growth. As soon as conditions alter so that a gain becomes more probable than a loss it is quickly discounted into a rise in the market price. Whilst there may exist considerable uncertainty concerning the future value, reflected in a large standard deviation around the mean, it is nonetheless the case that the optimal expectation will be the expectation of no change in existing values. It is perhaps important to note precisely the meaning of optimal in the present context. It is not meant to imply that the future value will necessarily ever coincide with the current valuation but only that expectations formed in this manner will minimize the degree to which expectations are subsequently proved false.

Thirdly, a great deal of economic analysis, and especially micro-economic analysis, is concerned not with absolute values as such but with comparative prices. For a great deal of economic theorising the absolute price level becomes an irrelevancy. If this is the case then the static expectations thesis gains in credibility for many comparative price ratios change but only gradually. This is particularly true with respect to the comparative prices of factor inputs where, in the absence of technological change, they display comparative stability over long periods. Indeed, many wage demands are geared to some concept of comparability between differing professional groups providing some institutional reinforcement to the comparative price stability generated by the market economy. Again, many prices are controlled by government agency and are thus rendered inflexible often over significant periods.

Examples include minimum wage controls, rent controls to protect tenants and certain product prices imposed to protect the interest of suppliers—witness the examples of EEC farm price controls. Here the current price is obviously the immediately expected future price and, in addition, serves to establish a benchmark against which future amendments to the prevailing controls are to be judged.

In the context of an inflationary setting, the static expectations thesis is often translated to mean that one's expectation today is that *real* values will be maintained in future periods. Thus the expectation is to the effect that all nominal values will adjust in line with the ongoing rate of inflation. Stated in this way, the static expectations thesis commands new respect. It remains a fact that under normal conditions real values change but relatively slowly. Today, modern trade unions display great sophistication and most wage claims are geared to recent inflationary experience which forms a basis for anticipating future inflation over the proposed period of the wage contract. Moreover, some incomes—old age pensions, civil service pensions and certain interest incomes from government bonds, for example—are effectively index linked to the appropriate index.

There are, therefore, many good reasons to conclude that the static expectations thesis is not without merit and indeed it possesses the great virtue of dealing with expectations explicitly as opposed to tacitly ignoring them. Nonetheless, in a world where nominal values are subject to fluctuations, often as a consequence of autonomous shocks or disturbances, it would appear deficient to neglect such disturbances completely in the formation of one's expectations. Thus, for example, the static expectations thesis postulates that the price of oil tomorrow will be equal to today's price, irrespective of today's announcement by OPEC ministers that they will take steps to curtail oil production. Moreover, whilst static expectations might be a reasonable postulate in market clearing conditions it is plainly inadequate in a world where false trading may be taking place.[1] This is most easily brought out by reference to the Cobweb theorem of price determination where suppliers respond to prices with a time lag but always with the expectation that prices prevailing today will prevail in the future period. The standard illustration is usually in terms of the traditional turkey farmer who brings his turkeys to market at Christmas or Thanksgiving but who requires a year's notice before he can alter the quantity of fattened turkeys he is able to market at either of these times. (We assume that frozen turkeys have yet to be invented.) His supply curve is accordingly two-dimensional. He has a market supply curve which is vertically sloped and indicates the stock of turkeys he can supply during the market period at Christmas or Thanksgiving, and he also has a longer-run supply curve showing his one-year lagged response to a price change. This situation is displayed in Figure 3.1 where we also assume a demand curve which generates a market clearing price/quantity combination P_1Q_1. This situation implies a stable equilibrium which, in the absence of any change, would imply the same quantity of turkeys, Q_1, being placed upon the market each year at the appropriate festival period. Suppose, however, that owing to some natural disaster such as pestilence or worse his stock of fattened turkeys is decimated just prior to the market period. The quantity he is able to bring to market is now accordingly Q_2 as indicated by the vertical market supply curve. Given the unchanged demand curve the market price soars to P_2 and, if we are to give any credence to the static expectations hypothesis, will generate the supply of turkeys indicated by Q_3 for the next market period when, in consequence, the market price will plummet to P_3 and generate a further supply response in the succeeding period. As is well known, the Cobweb theorem of price determination generates either a divergent or convergent price movement away from or towards the market clearing price depending upon the respective slopes of the supply and demand schedules.[2] Regardless of the outcome predicted by the theory, however, it should be clear that the static expectations thesis employed here fails totally as a description of reality. No turkey farmer would be so myopic as to behave in the manner indicated and even if he did he would surely learn from past experience and modify his behaviour accordingly. The overriding weakness of the hypothesis springs from the assumption that only current prices condition expectations of the prices to prevail in the subsequent period. Experience of what actually happened one period or two

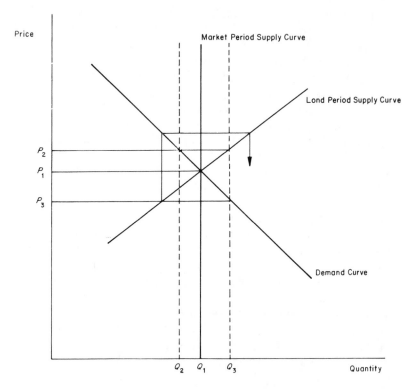

Figure 3.1. The Cobweb Theorem of Price Determination with Static Expectations

periods ago is not permitted to enter as a determinant in the formation of current expectations. The static expectations individual not only suffers from myopia but also from an extreme form of amnesia. Clearly, as a description of the way expectations are formed in volatile market conditions such behaviour is far removed from reality.

The static expectations thesis can be modelled more formally. Let us assume that expectations of future values are formed with a one-period lag. Then where P^e refers to the expected value (price) and P the actual value (price) and the time period is denoted by the subscript t, then at time $t-1$ we have

$$P_t^e = P_{t-1}$$

and at time t we have

$$P_{t+1}^e = P_t$$

and it follows that we have no necessary relationship between P_{t+1}^e and P_{t-1}.

ADAPTIVE EXPECTATIONS

By far the best known of expectational theories is that of adaptive expectations first modelled by Cagan (1956) within the context of a hyperinflationary setting. In conditions of hyperinflation it becomes virtually nonsensical to assume that individuals will not be influenced by past experience and in particular by the painful experience of how previous expectations have been proved false. The doctrine of adaptive expectations simply implies that economic agents will adapt their expectations in the light of past experience and that in particular they will learn from their mistakes.

The adaptive expectations approach can be formally modelled in the following way. At time t, let P_{t+1}^e be the price expected to prevail in the subsequent period. If P represents the actual price prevailing in the period denoted by the subscript then we have

$$P_{t+1}^e = P_t^e + \alpha[P_t - P_t^e] \ (0 < \alpha < 1).$$

That is to say, the price expected next period is equal to the price which had been expected for the current period plus some fraction of the extent that this expectation proved incorrect. To illustrate, with the value of α let us say equal to 0.5, if today's price is 100 whilst the expectation of today's price one period ago was 90, then today's expectation of price next period will be 95.

The same formula, of course, applies to all other periods. Thus,

$$P_t^e = P_{t-1}^e + \alpha[P_{t-1} - P_{t-1}^e]$$

and

$$P^e_{t-1} = P^e_{t-2} + \alpha[P_{t-2} - P^e_{t-2}]$$

and so forth. It follows that one's expectation of the price to prevail in the subsequent period is influenced by the expectations held in all past periods. However, as long as α is assumed to lie between the values of 0 and 1, the more distant the period the weaker will be the influence extended by that period upon the current price expectation. The argument here is not unlike the argument underlying the permanent income thesis of consumption behaviour where past income streams condition the expectation of permanent income but more distant income streams exert comparatively minor effect. We can illustrate this situation in the present context with an elementary example. In Table 3.1, for example, we again assume for simplicity an alpha coefficient of 0.5 and use P to denote the price level actually attained in the relevant period and P^e the price level that had been expected to prevail in the relevant period. Then if at time $t-3$ the expected price level had been 100, whereas in fact it turned out to be 110, then in period $t-2$ the expectation must be for the price level 105. If again the actual level turned out to be, let us say, 125, then the expectation for the period $t-1$ must be for 115. If the expectation is proved incorrect so that the price level 155 attains then the expectation for time period t would be for 135. And so forth; with the actual price level in period t of 185 the expectation for period $t+1$ becomes 160. Thus the expectation of the price level to prevail in period $t-3$ (i.e., the expectation

Table 3.1. Adaptive Price Expectations Formation $(\alpha = 0.5)$

Period	P^e (Expected Price)	P (Actual Price)
$t+1$	160	—
t	135	185
$t-1$	115	155
$t-2$	105	125
$t-3$	100	110

actually formed in period $t - 4$) does enter as an argument in the expectation formed in period t with respect to the price level expected to prevail in period $t + 1$. Given the alpha value of 0.5, however, its influence will be but one-eighth of the influence exerted by the expectation actually formed in period t. The influence of past expectations, therefore, wanes geometrically with the passage of time.

The adaptive expectations thesis is not without merit. It provides a fairly simple means of modelling expectations in economic theory whilst postulating a mode of behaviour upon the part of economic agents which seems eminently sensible. The belief that people learn from experience is obviously a more sensible starting point than the implicit assumption that they are totally devoid of memory, characteristic of the static expectations thesis. Moreover, the assertion that more distant experiences exert a lesser effect than more recent experience would accord with common sense and would appear to be amply confirmed by simple observation. In addition, the adaptive expectations thesis does generate certain results which are intuitively appealing. Thus, for example, if a price level has prevailed over a reasonable period of time it will inevitably become the price level expected to prevail in the immediate future. The adaptive expectations thesis will progressively generate this expectation. Again, if the price level is suddenly disturbed, let us say by a once and for all tax change, and then settles down to its new level over a peiod of time, the adaptive expectations postulate suggests that economic agents' expectations will progressively approximate the new value. Moreover, this approximation to the new actual value will be generated in a relatively brief time. To see this, consider a good whose price level is 100 and has been held stable over a considerable period. At time t, the price level expected to prevail at time $t + 1$ will accordingly be 100. Suppose, however, that at time t a 50 per cent tax is imposed which, passed forward in its entirety, raises the price to 150. Assuming the new price remains unchanged, how long will it take for the adaptive expectations thesis to generate the expectations of the actual price prevailing? The answer, somewhat disturbingly, is forever and a day for in truth the adaptive expectations thesis will never generate a price of expectation of 150 as long as α is less

28

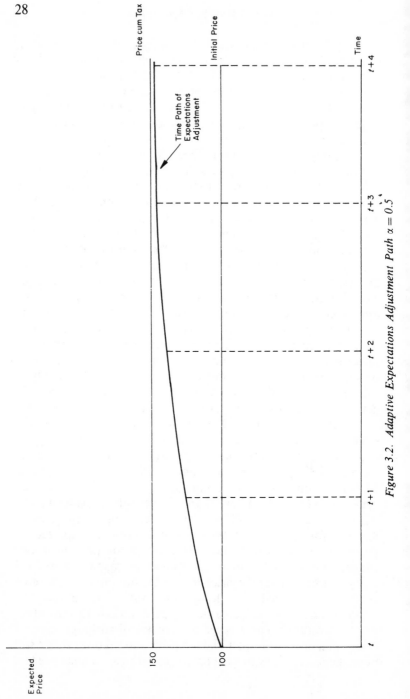

Figure 3.2. *Adaptive Expectations Adjustment Path* α = 0.5

than one. Whilst this is perhaps an unfortunate consequence of the adaptive expectations formulation it is nonetheless true that a fairly close approximation to the new price will be achieved relatively quickly. In Figure 3.2, for example, again assuming an α coefficient of 0.5 we show that an expected price of 146.875 is attained by the end of period four.

For expositional purposes we have adopted an α coefficient of 0.5. There is no reason why α should be held constant however. It seems reasonable to assume that α will be relatively larger in periods of relatively volatile price changes and relatively smaller during periods of relative price stability. Incorporating this behavioural assumption into the adaptive expectations thesis does improve the overall plausibility of the doctrine.

However, there exists one fundamental objection to the adaptive expectations hypothesis which, in the opinion of rational expectation theorists, renders it a decidedly suboptimal mode of behaviour. The objection is simply this: it ignores the facts of the current situation in a most alarming way. Thus, for example, and in keeping with our previous illustration, economic agents are held to take into account the current price and the extent to which their former expectation is proved false in forming their expectation of the future price, but to ignore entirely the announcement of the imposition of a 50 per cent tax levy. Agents with adaptive expectations are held to be sufficiently sophisticated to learn from past mistakes yet amazingly myopic with respect to the impact of current exogenous shocks to the system. Not only are extraneous shocks discounted, they are in fact ignored entirely. As a description of actual behaviour this aspect of the adaptive expectations thesis is far removed from reality. Moreover, whilst such a view of price expectations formation would be reasonably satisfactory in a world of relatively infrequent tax changes, import price changes and similar once and for all impacts, it is a far less satisfactory explanation of expectations formation in conditions of continuous inflation. In particular if inflation is accelerating—that is to say, if price increases are occurring at an increasing rate—then the adaptive expectations doctrine will perform badly and will persistently understate the rate of price increase. In fact, in the accelerating inflationary conditions which prevailed in the late 1960s and early 1970s, the trade unions showed remarkable sophistication in national wage negotiations, not only in anticipating future inflation rates but also in calculating the effects of inflation in pushing wage earners into high tax brackets and depleting real take-home pay. This experience served to discredit the adaptive expectations approach and was doubtless instrumental in promoting the conversion to rational expectations.

KEYNES AND EXPECTATIONS

There can be no doubt that over the past ten or fifteen years the character of macro-economics has changed and in particular the dominance of Keynesian macro-economics has been eroded both in theoretical debate and in policy prescription. In part, this development stems from an increasing awareness of the inadequacy of the micro-economic underpinnings of the *General Theory*, from the rise of monetarism in inflationary conditions and from the recent poor record of demand management policies in being able to attain full employment output levels. All of these developments have been intimately linked with the rise of rational expectations; indeed, in some respects they have provided the impetus to rational expectations philosophy whilst in others they reflect the consequences of rational expectations conclusions. Certainly, Keynesian oriented demand management policies have been called into question particularly by the startling claim that consistent countercyclical policy will be ineffectual in influencing real output and employment *even in the short run*.

It is, therefore, appropriate to enquire as to the manner in which Keynes dealt with expectations and how his treatment differs from that of the rational expectations school. This question would be of interest in its own right, but it has recently received added emphasis in a paper by Begg (1982a) which makes the remarkable claim that the *General Theory* anticipates much of the recent work on rational expectations.

One of Keynes' achievements was to recognise that meaningful macro-economic theory would need to incorporate the role of expectations. Indeed, the evolution of Keynes' thinking on monetary economics was marked by the increasing recognition of the importance of expectations in determining the eventual outcome. In the *Tract on Monetary Reform* (1923), for example, Keynes put forward a straightforward statement of the quantity theory of money, very much in the Cambridge tradition, and in no way at variance with the famous equation of exchange which Irving Fisher had propounded more than a decade previously. Even here, however, Keynes recognised the importance of expectations. Very much influenced by the experience of the recent German inflation, Keynes argued that inflationary experiences could condition expectations of further inflation which would exert a feedback effect upon the demand for cash holdings and the demand for bank deposits. The induced increase in velocity so obtained would serve to fuel the inflationary process still further and generate still further expectations of future inflationary trends. Likewise, in the celebrated *Treatise on Money* (1930) expectations with regard to future bond and securities prices emerge as a determinant of the rate of interest which, in turn, exercises decisive influence upon inflationary and deflationary oscillations within the economy. It is in the *General Theory*, however, that the Keynesian treatment of expectations culminates in such pessimistic conclusions. Essentially the concern is with *inconsistencies* in expectations between different economic agents as, for example, between savers and investors, and with the *volatility* of expectations concerning the *future expectations of others*. It is this latter consideration which dominates Keynes' thinking and which forms the basis of his business cycle theory. More importantly, however, it also contributes to Begg's interpretation that Keynes believed that expectations cannot be sensibly incorporated into economic models as endogenous variables. This is an issue to which we shall return. For the moment it is perhaps instructive to enquire how Keynes thought expectations were formed in practice.

The Keynesian position is to assert that with regard to economic affairs 'knowledge of the future is fluctuating, vague and uncertain.' Moreover, returning to a theme which Keynes had explored in his influential *A Treatise on Probability* (1921), the assertion is made that the uncertain economic future is not one about which reasonable calculations can be made. Unlike a game of poker, for example, where one can evaluate the chances of completing a straight flush, or alternatively a public lottery where one can determine with reasonable exactitude the chances of having one's ticket drawn, there exists no scientific basis to form any calculable probability whatsoever with respect to, say, the price of tin in twenty years' time. Unlike a game of poker, the price of tin will be influenced by *unique* events, such as invention and technical innovation or by the advent of war. There is no way in which meaningful probabilities can be assigned to such possible outcomes.

It is arguable that Keynes took a too pessimistic view in claiming that no basis existed for applying probability theory to uncertain future economic outcomes, but, given this presumption, a number of conclusions follow. Individuals, unable to assess probabilities in some rational manner, fall back upon expediency. In particular, they tend to accept current trends and valuations as a reliable guide to the future and assume that the existing prices of capital assets accurately reflect their true future discounted income yields. Moreover, in a world of uncertainty, there is an undeniable tendency to follow the majority view and accept the conventional wisdom. Expectations formed in this manner and based upon such flimsy real evidence of the future are subject to sudden and often violent change as a by-product of panic fears and rumours which may possess no basis in fact. The precarious nature of long-term expectation is enhanced by the increasing tendency in modern economies towards a division between the ownership and the management of equity. Increasingly, ownership is concentrated into the hands of people who lack any real knowledge of the business in question and who have no real basis for attaching a valuation to the assets involved. Furthermore, the activities of speculators on the stock market, who are concerned not with the true valuation of an asset but rather with the valuation to be attached by the stock market in the near future, mean that securities are often unrealistically priced and give rise to quite unrealistic expectations of the true value of similar assets. Sooner or later, however, the true values must become apparent to even the most optimistic investor and when this occurs a sudden crisis in confidence can develop. Periods of excessive over-optimism and excessive over-pessimism alternate and expectations in general are extremely volatile. Indeed, it is extreme uncertainty about the future which accounts for liquidity preference and which explains the alleged interest elasticity of the overall demand for money.

The activity of professionals operating in financial markets, such as the stock exchange, is of crucial importance to the Keynesian theory, and carries implications for rational expectations formation. The energies and skills of the professional speculator are concerned 'not with making superior long-term forecasts of the probable yield of an investment over its whole life, but with foreseeing changes in the conventional basis of valuation a short time ahead of the general public.' Hence the professional is concerned with obtaining and processing information which allows him to anticipate possible changes in the psychology of the market. Keynes' own metaphor from the *General Theory* summarises the essence of this activity vividly:

professional investment may be likened to those newspaper competitions in which the competitors have to pick out the six prettiest faces from a hundred photographs, the prize being awarded to the competitor whose choice most nearly corresponds to the average preferences of the competitors as a whole; so that each competitor has to pick, not those faces which he himself finds prettiest, but those which he thinks likeliest to catch the fancy of the other competitors, all of whom are looking at the problem from the same point of view. It is not a case of choosing those which, to the best of one's judgement, are really the prettiest, nor even those which average opinion genuinely thinks the prettiest. We have reached the third degree where we devote our intelligences to anticipating what average opinion expects the average opinion to be. And there are some, I believe, who practise the fourth fifth and higher degrees (p. 156).

Keynes' conclusion, to follow Begg's interpretation, is to suggest that expectations are virtually incapable of being dealt with in the context of a formal economic model as endogenous variables. Expectations derived as the 'outcome of the mass psychology of a large number of ignorant individuals are liable to change violently as the result of a sudden fluctuation of opinion due to factors which do not really make much difference to the prospective yield' and do not lend themselves to endogenous treatment, but have to be imposed upon the model as an exogenous shift parameter. Recognition of the exogeneity of Keynesian expectations makes the Keynesian model far more plausible. If expectations are exogenous and *fixed* in the short run, then it is reasonable to proxy permanent income by current income. Likewise, if net prospective income streams from capital assets are held constant, the determining factor in investment spending becomes the rate of interest. In the same way, if expectations of future bond prices are held constant then the demand for asset cash will be determined by the current interest rate. In short, many of the post-Keynesian 'improvements' to the *General Theory* are already accounted for by the assumption of exogenous and temporary fixed expectations. At the same time, the possibility of autonomous shifts in expectations, especially with respect to future profits, plays an important role in generating the comparative static adjustment which moves the economy from one equilibrium to another.

Of course, the adoption of exogenous expectations begs many questions. Speculators holding idle cash balances in the expectation that interest rates will rise in the future continue to do so, in the absence of some autonomous disturbance, no matter how long the interest rate remains unchanged. Surely it would be more reasonable to posit that the concept of a 'normal' rate of interest would itself be a function of the interval of time that elapsed with the interest rate held constant, i.e., the expected rate of interest would become endogenous. Whilst arguments of this nature possess validity, the adoption of the assumption of exogeneity is a useful approximation which renders the theory far more tractable if also empirically empty.

This interpretation of Keynes' treatment of expectations concludes with an interesting speculation. It suggests that Keynes may have confused the possibility of modelling expectations with the possibility of modelling changes in expectations. In Begg's view, the rational expectations hypothesis provides a neat solution to Keynes' dilemma; it permits an explanation of the current state of expectations whilst simultaneously denying that future revisions to those expectations could be accurately foreseen. If Keynes' 'given state of expectation' is taken to be equivalent to the current rational expectation of the future progress of the economy, prices, and so forth, then in this view, the entire analysis of expectations in the *General Theory* could be restated in terms of rational expectations.

NOTES

1 False trading refers to the existence of exchange taking place at prices other than those which equate supply and demand, i.e., at non-equilibrium prices. Whilst largely excluded in elementary expositions of price theory, in all probability it is a relatively common phenomenon in the real world.
2 The dividing case, that of equal slopes of the supply and demand curves, generates a continuously oscillating price movement around the market clearing price.

4 The Expectations Augmented Phillips Curve

Keynesian oriented economists relied, for many of their policy prognostications, upon the belief in the existence of a fairly stable relationship between output and inflation summarised in the familiar concept of the Phillips Curve. Providing that this relationship was indeed stable, then the authorities were granted a menu of policy choice. By intervening to alter the level of aggregate demand they could trade off higher levels of employment at the cost of greater inflation and *vice versa*.

Monetarist critics of the Phillips Curve, particularly Friedman (1968) and Phelps (1967), denied the existence of this stable relationship and concluded instead that the trade-off was largely fictitious and of temporary duration only. In this view the economy would exhibit an inherent tendency to gravitate towards its '*natural*' (near full employment) level of output if left to its own devices, and this 'natural' level determined by real forces operating in the economy was quite independent of the inflation rate which, in turn, was determined by the rate of change in the nominal money stock.

Initially this denial of the Keynesian policy prescription was based upon the assumption of an adaptive expectations approach upon the part of labour in negotiating national wage agreements. This leads logically to the assertion that the long-run Phillips Curve will be considerably more steeply sloped than the short-term Phillips Curve, thus minimising the long-term trade-off, and that in the extreme case it would be vertical above the natural level of employment thus denying any long-term trade-off whatsoever. Nonetheless, some scope for countercyclical policy will remain in the short term given the adaptive expectations thesis with regard to trade union behaviour in wage negotiations. Rational expectation theory is in large measure a reaction against this conclusion. Initially, therefore, it is useful to examine the implications of the Phillips Curve analysis when modified by the doctrine of adaptive expectations to understand fully why rational expectations theorists regard it as an inferior form of expectations formation.

Let us assume that both labour demand and labour supply are a function of the real wage rate. Let us also assume, however, that labour demand is a function of the money wage rate deflated by the *actual* price index, whereas the labour supply is a function of the money wage rate deflated by the price level *expected* to prevail when the wage bargain is initially struck. It follows that if actual prices and expected prices diverge then it is possible to generate a position of disequilibrium in the labour market. If a disequilibrium situation does occur in the labour market, then it is possible for the actual amount of output and employment to deviate from its 'natural' market clearing level at least over the period of the wage contract. It is upon the ability of the authorities to generate such disequilibrium situations in the labour market that the scope for discretionary interventionist fine tuning policies ultimately depends.

In order to pursue this analysis consider the Phillips Curve depicted in Figure 4.1. With the unemployment level OQ we have the inflation rate of 5 per cent. Let us assume that this inflation rate has been experienced for some time and was the expected rate of inflation at the time labour negotiated its wage contract at the employment level OQ. Let us now invoke the adaptive expectations thesis, but for simplicity let us assume the value of α to be equal to one. Under the present assumptions, therefore, the expected inflation rate is 5 per cent and this is the figure that trade unions will adopt when bargaining over their real wage in the next contract period. Presumably this rate of inflation and the given amount of employment OQ can continue indefinitely. Let us assume,

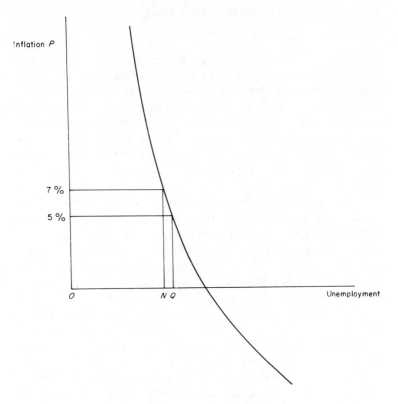

Figure 4.1. Phillips Curve

however, that for electoral reasons the government expands employment by generating upward pressure on wages in the labour market so that as unemployment declines inflation rises as predicted by the Phillips Curve. Suppose unemployment falls to *ON* as inflation rises to 7 per cent. What are the consequences?

Labour perceives a decline in its real wage over the period of contract since actual inflation now exceeds that expected. When renegotiating its contract, therefore, it will attempt to restore the former real wage for the given amount of unemployment *OQ*. In doing so, it will take account of the past expectation of current inflation and the extent to which this was shown to be incorrect. Accordingly,

$$P^e = 5 + 1[7 - 5] = 7\%$$

At the start of the new contract period, therefore, labour will bargain for a wage which will restore its former real wage at the employment level OQ with the expectation of future inflation rates of 7 per cent. The net effect is to shift the Phillips Curve to the right so that the combination OQ of unemployment and 7 per cent inflation now prevails. The outward shift of the Phillips Curve eliminates the initial trade-off. Initially, at the start of the contract period labour's assumption appears correct.

Suppose, however, that as a consequence of this higher nominal wage level inflation rises above the expected 7 per cent. Once again, over the contract period, labour's real wage will be eroded, the demand for labour will be extended and once again we obtain a trade-off between the two competing goals of policy. Unemployment falls below OQ as inflation climbs above 7 per cent. Once again, however, this situation will be short lived. When labour comes to renegotiate its contract it will again attempt to restore its original real wage associated with the unemployment level OQ and in doing so it will invoke an inflation expectation equal to the current rate. Each new contract period will see an outward shift of the Phillips relation. Ultimately, over the long term, such a process will generate an infinite number of short-run Phillips Curves intersecting a vertical permanent Phillips relation at the natural level of employment OQ, as depicted in Figure 4.2. The alleged trade-off available to the authorities, therefore, is of short-term duration only and arises solely because the postulated expectational behaviour fails to deal adequately with *accelerating* rates of inflation.

Now the crucial issue in this analysis turns upon the question of how well labour anticipates the future level of inflation. If expectations are formed adaptively and the value of the coefficient α is equal to one, then the disequilibrium situation is eliminated at the start of each contract period.

In this situation, the long-term trade-off disappears as the long-run Phillips Curve becomes vertical; at the end of each contract period a new wage deal is negotiated based upon the

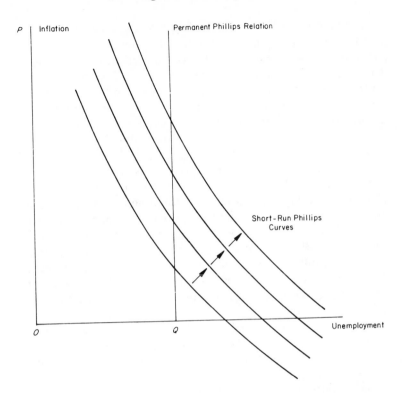

Figure 4.2. Long-run and Short-run Phillips Curves

premise that the price level prevailing will continue into the future. In negotiating the new contract the former real wage will be restored at the prevailing price level for the original amount of unemployment *OQ*. The Phillips Curve is thus shifted upwards so as to maintain real wages constant at the *start* of each contract period. However, a short-term trade-off can still remain. One of the failings of the adaptive expectations thesis is that it does not perform well in conditions of accelerating inflation. It is entirely backward looking and fails to take account of the fact that the nominal wage increase needed to restore the former real wage will generate further price inflation not anticipated by the adaptive expectations doctrine.

If the alpha coefficient is less than one, then whilst the long-run Phillips Curve will be more steeply sloped than the short-run curve, it will never in fact become vertical, implying that the authorities maintain a permanent ability to trade-off output and inflation. This arises because with the assumption of α less than one, labour never succeeds under the adaptive expectations thesis in restoring its original level of real wages.

We are now in a position to understand the objections to the adaptive expectations thesis raised by the proponents of rational expectations. Even with the assumption of an α coefficient equal to one, implying the absence of money illusion, the adaptive expectations hypothesis is asserting that the economic agent formulating his expectations in this way will systematically understate the degree of future inflation and will persistently enter into contracts which are ultimately found wanting in failing to maintain his real income. Surely if this is the case, he will sooner or later modify his behaviour. His manner of expectations formation is persistently being proved incorrect and, moreover, not only incorrect but always biased to his detriment. It is not a case of gaining on the swings what one loses on the roundabout; our adaptive expectations agent never gets off the roundabout. The rational expectations doctrine is thus based upon perhaps the oldest premise in the subject matter of economics, namely that individual economic agents will behave in a manner consistent with maximising their wellbeing. To continue to pursue adaptive expectations formation and to be continually disappointed by the outcome in a systematic manner would be tantamount to pursuing non-maximising behaviour. Finally, as Laidler has emphasised (1982), there are no information costs involved in learning that his expectational behaviour is suboptimal. The information is generated as a natural by-product of his day to day market activity.

It is perhaps instructive to summarise the essence of the preceding argument in terms of conventional aggregate supply and demand analysis which permits us to perceive more readily the scope for interventionist monetary and fiscal policies. In Figure 4.3 let us posit an initial situation of price level P_1 and real output Q_1 determined by the intersection of the aggregate demand schedule AD^1 with *both* the positively sloped short-

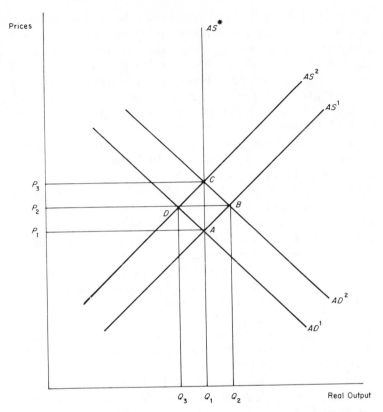

Figure 4.3. Adaptive Expectations and the Short-Run and Long-Run Response of Aggregate Supply

run aggregate supply curve AS^1 and the long-run vertical aggregate supply curve which we denote by AS^*. Q_1 is accordingly the *natural* level of output. Implicit in the following argument is again the assumption that real wage rates govern the demand for labour so that employers perceive any increase in prices as a decrease in the real wage rate and extend their demand accordingly, whereas employees suffer from a temporary form of money illusion and fail to perceive that real wages have declined—at least initially. In such a situation an increase in the level of aggregate demand from AD^1 to AD^2, brought about by appropriate demand management strategies, will generate an increase in prices towards P_2. The decline in real wages extends the demand for labour as employment and output both respond, given the assumption of money illusion upon the part of employees. We thus move along the positively sloped AS^1 curve from point A to point B and output expands to Q_2. Once again we are in the world of trade-off with higher output and employment levels being purchased at the cost of higher prices. However, again it is reasonable to suppose that this situation will be but short lived. Once it is realised that the real wage has fallen in the move from A to B, employees will act to restore their former real wage. This will imply an upward shift of the AS^1 schedule towards AS^2 as workers attempt to relate their former labour supply to the former real wage. In the process, output and employment will contract along AD^2 and if this adjustment is complete—that is to say, if the former real wage is fully restored—it will only come to an end at the original output level Q_1. The total adjustment to the expansion of aggregate demand thus comprises the short-run movement from A to B together with the long-term movement B to C. The only long-term consequence of the expansionary demand management policy is to generate an increase in the price level to P_3 with output and employment unchanged at their natural levels.

Precisely similar reasoning is involved in the reverse case of a fall in aggregate demand generated by contractionary monetary and fiscal policies. Commencing with the price output combination P_3Q_1 a decrease in aggregate demand would shift the AD^2 schedule downwards to AD^1. Prices fall from P_3 towards P_2 and real wages increase in consequence. This increase in real wages is perceived by employers and the demand for labour contracts, revealed in a movement along the aggregate supply schedule AS^2 from C to D as output falls below its natural level to Q_3. Again, however, this situation is short lived. Once labour perceives the change in its real income the aggregate supply schedule AS^2 will shift downwards to AS^1, implying the movement from D to A along the aggregate demand schedule AD^1. Again, the net effect of the contractionary macro-economic policy has no long-term impact upon the natural level of output and employment.

This line of analysis suggests that both positively sloped and vertical aggregate supply schedules co-exist. In the short run the aggregate supply schedule is positively sloped because those agents supplying labour services respond only gradually to the changes in nominal prices. In the context of the adaptive expectations thesis it is possible for the adjustment never to be completed if the α coefficient falls below one. The adoption of the vertical long-run aggregate supply curve is really an acceptance that the coefficient will to all intents and purposes equal one. Agents will act so as to restore their former level of real wages and the long-run supply curve will be vertical above the natural level of output. This conclusion is obviously relevant to the entire issue of supply side economics; if aggregate demand management policies cannot affect the permanent level of output then perhaps the emphasis should be directed towards appropriate *micro-economic* policies aimed at bringing about a desirable outward shift of the vertical aggregate supply schedule to raise natural levels of output and employment.

Nonetheless, as long as the short-run supply schedule remains positively sloped some scope for demand management policies must remain as a short-term palliative. It is precisely this contention that the rational expectations school has sought to deny. Arguing that the expectations mechanism incorporated into adaptive expectations is deficient and hence suboptimal and inconsistent with maximising behaviour, it argues that when expectations are formed rationally changes in aggregate demand may not even influence output and employment in the short run. Indeed, the logic of this thesis is to deny the distinction between the long run and the short providing we are willing to discount the costs associated with making the required adjustments. In practice, of course, adjustment costs may be sizeable, as we shall argue in the next chapter.

5 The Meaning of Rational Expectations

It is now time to define precisely what is meant, and perhaps more importantly what is not meant, by the doctrine of rational expectations. First and foremost, it assumes that individual economic agents use *current available* and *relevant* information in forming their expectations and do not rely purely upon past experience. Thus, for example, an OPEC announcement to cut the price of oil, or a government announcement to increase the rate of tax upon oil, will be taken into account in forming one's expectation of the future price of oil, *in addition* to recent and more distant observations concerning oil price movements. Secondly, it is assumed that this information is then processed and analysed in an optimal and efficient manner in order to arrive at an intelligent estimate or expectation of the value to be taken by the economic variable under consideration.[1]

Now it is important to note what is not implied in these dual statements. First, they need not imply that individuals will utilise *all* possible relevant information. Certain information will be costly to acquire. Likewise, it need not imply that the information used will be subject to intensive scrutiny or analysis. Most economic agents do not possess elaborate home computers upon which they perform nightly simulations invoking large-scale econometric models of the economy. Again, a cost is implied in the very processing of information and not least the cost of the time and effort involved. Instead, what is being asserted is that individuals will acquire and process information in as intelligent a manner as possible, as

47

long as the perceived marginal benefits from so doing (in terms of an improved expectation of the future or an expectation held with greater certainty) exceed the marginal cost of acquiring and processing the relevant information.

We may summarise this assertion with the aid of Figure 5.1. It is reasonable to assume that certain information will be attained at virtually zero cost and other information will be attained at minimal cost—for example, information provided in newspapers, radio broadcasts and so forth. Beyond a point, however, more specialist information will become increasingly

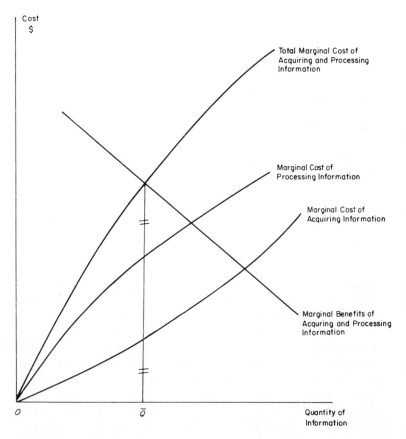

Figure 5.1. Rational expectations and the Optimal Quantity of Information

more difficult and expensive to acquire and may involve outlays on expensive books, periodicals and even professional consultancy services in the case of financial and commodity markets. Hence we posit that the marginal cost of acquiring information will be upward sloping as depicted in Figure 5.1. There will also be costs associated with the processing of the information so obtained. Again we can imagine that the marginal cost of analysing information will increase as the total amount of information increases, requiring the invocation of more elaborate theoretical structures although here there may be significant economies of scale.[2] Nonetheless, let us assume that the total marginal cost of both acquiring and processing relevant information is positively sloped as indicated in the figure. The marginal benefits associated with the acquisition and analysis of this information are, of course, determined by the subjective evaluation of the economic agent. It would seem reasonable, however, to assume that the curve relating to the marginal benefits of collecting and analysing relevant information will be negatively sloped as indicated. Consider, for example, an agent involved in dealings in a futures commodity market such as coffee and needing information on current output yields in order to form an expectation over future coffee prices. Clearly, he would need information from the world's major coffee producing nations; beyond this, however, additional information concerning the output yields of the relatively minor coffee producing nations would be of progressively diminishing significance to the formulation of future price expectation.

The situation portrayed in Figure 5.1 suggests that maximising behaviour would dictate that the amount of information acquired and analysed would be $O\bar{Q}$, and this amount would differ for different individual agents according to their own particular circumstances. Somebody engaged in futures commodity markets, for example, would presumably acquire considerably more information and subject it to more sophisticated analysis than someone who is retired on an index linked pension.

All that the rational expectations thesis implies, therefore, is that individuals will collect and analyse a determinate amount of information in formulating their expectations if they are welfare maximisers. Since they do not utilise all information and since any information will be subject to a certain degree of uncertainty, it does not imply anything about perfect foresight. Nor does it imply that rational expectations will always be correct. Indeed, on occasions, the rational expectation may be outperformed *ex post* by alternative modes of expectations formation, although it is formally true that the variance of the rational expectation prediction will be less than that possessed by alternative specifications. However, what is claimed by the rational expectations theorist is that individual economic agents will not make *systematic* expectational errors indefinitely. That is to say, individuals will learn from past experiences and will be able to eliminate any regularities in their expectational errors (systematic errors) from their future expectations formation. What is implied here is that ultimately whatever errors remain will be essentially *random* errors which are uncorrelated with the information obtained and processed. To illustrate, consider the individual who observes an increase in money supply growth but takes no account of it in his expectation of price level changes. His expectation is subsequently shown to be incorrect in that he understates the increase in the price level. If this experience is repeated time and again, each time with the agent's expectations being shown to be *systematically* incorrect, he will ultimately learn from experience and modify his process of expectations formation. Ultimately, he will begin to act so as to foresee the effect of monetary change upon the price level. Now in the event his expectation may be shown to be widely inaccurate; in the case of some natural disaster such as earthquake or pestilence his expectations may be shown to be a gross understatement of the actual price level change. But the expectations error will be essentially random and unrelated, statistically speaking, to the available information at the time the expectation was made.

Nor does the rational expectations thesis imply that all economic agents have an intricate knowledge of economics and carry with them a detailed model of how the economy actually behaves. Some may, of course, possess such a model, but the vast majority of economic agents do not and it is a gross distortion of rational expectations theory to maintain that this is an essential ingredient of the hypothesis. All that is being claimed is that *consciously or otherwise* individuals will begin to predict the consequences of a given change in the light of their past observed experiences and in so doing they will begin to eliminate systematic expectational errors. It is a short step from the above to the proposition that economic agents will learn to anticipate systematic macro-economic policy changes and in so doing will be able to modify their behaviour so as to neutralise or counter the intended effect of such changes. Suppose, for example, that economic agents learn from experience that the money supply is always increased when the unemployment level exceeds a certain percentage and further that when the money supply increases price increases follow in roughly similar magnitude. If they now observe unemployment passing the critical level, they will anticipate the money supply increase and form an expectation of the subsequent price rise which they will take into account in modifying their behaviour. In doing so, they will neutralise the effect of the money supply change upon real variables. Recall the illustration we employed in chapter 1. Our debtors and creditors anticipating the price effects of the impending money supply change adjust nominal interest rates upwards, thus negating any impact upon the real rate of interest. Of course, this argument refers only to the money supply change which is anticipated. It may be that the money supply change encompasses both an anticipated component and a random component which agents are unable to predict, so that the random component catches economic agents unaware and generates real effects.

We have argued that individual economic agents do not need to possess a complex model of the economy in order to learn to avoid making systematic expectational errors. Instead, they may simply learn from previous experience and modify their behaviour accordingly. However, a crucial distinction arises for the policy implications of the rational expectations thesis if we assume that agents do possess a formal model as opposed to the case where they rely solely upon historical experience. To make this point in an admittedly *simpliste* manner, let us assume that the appropriate model of the economy is given by the equation of exchange

$$MV = PQ$$

where the symbols have the same meaning as before. Let us also assume that in all past periods V and Q have remained constant, with the result that any increase in the money supply will automatically translate into an equal percentage increase in prices. The economic agent relying solely upon historical experience will always expect a money supply increase to imply a future price increase without exception.

In contrast, assume an economic agent fully understands the quantity theory model of the economy summarised in the equation of exchange. If he is informed that the government intends to increase the money supply by 10 per cent but at the same time it is announced that some autonomous discovery (say, North Sea oil) has increased output by 10 per cent, then he will logically be led to conclude that there will be no impact upon prices. This distinction is important because a change of government (or even a change of the Minister of Finance, to refer back to our illustration of Chapter 1) might signal a different systematic response to a given economic indicator. A Labour or Democratic administration, for example, might respond in a totally different manner to a given set of unemployment figures as compared to a Conservative or Republican administration. For the economic agent who fully understands how the economy actually operates such a change would be of no consequence. He would simply observe the actions of the existing administration regardless of its political hue and incorporate them into his formal model of the economy to obtain a correct expectation of future economic variables. In contrast, the agent lacking a formal theoretical framework and relying solely upon the historical record would suddenly find himself involved in expectational error. One is reminded of Bertrand Russell's fable of the chicken warning of the dangers of attaching too much importance to simple correlation. The sun rises in the morning and the farmer comes out to feed the chicken. The next day the same pattern is repeated, and so on. The chicken learns to associate the rising of the sun with the appearance of the benevolent farmer bringing food, until one day when the sun rises and the chicken comes forth to greet the farmer who promptly wrings its neck. This is an example of expectational error arising from a failure upon the part of the chicken to understand fully the formal model underlying the behaviour of the farmer. The economic agent depending solely upon the historical record will find himself involved in expectational error; however, such errors will be systematic and ultimately will be corrected in the light of experience.[3] However, this relearning process could take considerable time and may still be incomplete when the next traumatic change takes place in the governing regime. The belief that expectational errors will be fully eliminated over time, as implied in the rational expectations hypothesis, does depend upon the assumption of a reasonable continuity in the policy prescription emanating from government.

We have argued that this world is peopled by two types of individuals, those who possess formal economic models of how the economy actually operates, and those who do not. It is reasonably safe to conclude that the latter will predominate and indeed will enjoy a fairly sizeable majority. The question which is crucial is whether this majority behaves in the way that the rational expectations theorists expect. Now in raising this issue, it is important to note that we are not concerned to refute the postulate of maximising behaviour upon which rational expectations theory depends. One can concede the maximising postulate and still question whether individual economic agents have the *ability* to learn from past experience so as to eliminate systematic expectational error.

Usually the rational expectations thesis is put forward in terms of a very simple mechanical quantity theory view. A readily observed change in the money stock is followed by a very similar change in the general level of prices. No other complications enter to fudge the issue. If the world were as simple as depicted here then it would be reasonable to conclude that all economic agents would adapt in the light of their experience. The degree of perception required to link monetary change with the price level would be on a par with that needed to associate a drop in temperature with nightfall.

However, the world is not so simple and there exists a danger in generalising from such simple mechanistic models. Far from monetary change being readily observable, there is considerable difficulty in determining what the money supply is and what is the appropriate definition of the money stock. In the United Kingdom, for example, the Conservative administration returned to power in 1979 linked its medium-term economic strategy to the M_3 definition of the money supply, whilst many economic commentators argued that the more appropriate definition to mirror the progress of the economy was the much narrower M_1 definition.[4] If professional economists can disagree as to what should constitute the appropriate definition of the money stock, how does the proverbial man in the street determine whether a money supply change has occurred or not? Again, whilst it may seem eminently reasonable to correct systematic errors in the light of experience when the same situation is repeated in *identical* circumstances again and again, in the real world the same situation never actually recurs. All sorts of highly complex interdependent changes occur in an economy over a passage of time so that a given situation can never actually be repeated. This means that the rational expectations thesis is demanding that economic agents possess an extremely sensitive and *selective* perception of the crucial changes in the economy even when they lack any formal training in economic science. It is a tall order and casual observation might suggest that few laymen will possess such ability.

This critique might be damning to the rational expectations thesis if it were assumed that economic agents formed their economic expectations in isolation. However, this is not the case. Unable to understand or fathom the all-important changes occurring in economic variables, they fall back upon the consensus of opinion reported in the news media. Indeed, for many people this will be the easiest and cheapest way of forming their expectations of key economic magnitudes. That the media do influence expectations significantly has been amply demonstrated time and again with reference to stock market fluctuations following press comment. Likewise, most economic agents will take account of the prevailing economic forecasts in forming their own expectations of the values of future economic variables. Such forecasts, of course, are prepared by people having a formal model of the economy, which they believe to be the 'true' model and which attempts to take account of all relevant information. Thus, economic agents forming their expectations rationally and possessed of a formal model of the economy condition the expectations of those agents who lack any formal economic training or model analysis. The latter agents, of course, are also forming their expectations rationally in the sense that they base expectations upon current information and learn, presumably, to correct systematic errors.

Finally, much of rational expectations theory is concerned with the behaviour of labour in negotiating formal wage contracts. Indeed, this aspect of rational expectations is central to the issue of the ability of the macro-authorities to be able to influence real variables. Now here, many economic agents will be willing to allow this bargaining process to be conducted by trade union leadership. In turn, the trade union leadership will pay very close attention to crucial economic variables in the economy. They will possess a highly sophisticated model of how the economy behaves and employ highly qualified economic advisors and it will pay them to obtain and analyse information and data far beyond those readily available to individual economic agents acting in isolation. Through the proxy of trade unions many economic agents are acting in accordance with the rational expectations postulate. The thesis cannot, therefore, be dismissed out of court, and to the extent that it is consistent with maximising behaviour, it must be judged superior to alternative methods of expectations formation. Despite all the limitations, therefore, it behoves us to examine some of the implications in greater detail.

NOTES

1   Rational expectations need not, of course, be confined to economic variables. One might invoke the thesis in forming an expectation of the outcome of the next election or indeed about next week's weather. For our purposes, however, we shall restrict ourselves solely to economic variables and normally, unless otherwise stated, we will be concerned with future price levels.

2   Strictly speaking, there will be a whole series of marginal cost curves relating to the acquisition and processing of information. The greater the certainty of the accuracy of the information acquired, and the more sophisticated its degree of analysis, the greater, *ceteris paribus*, will be the marginal cost. For simplicity we have ignored this complication here but clearly it is relevant to the optimal amount of information which individuals will collect and process.

3 Sadly, not in the case of Russell's chicken.
4 The M_3 definition of the money supply is much broader than the M_1 definition because it includes not just notes and coins in circulation but also bank deposits. When interest rates are rising rapidly, individuals have the incentive to economise upon their cash holdings and transfer money into interest yielding bank deposits. The M_1 definition of the money supply might be contracting whilst the M_3 definition might be expanding, giving contradictory impressions of the future progress of the economy.

APPENDIX: MUTHIAN RATIONAL EXPECTATIONS

The rational expectations doctrine was first introduced into economics by Muth (1961), although it was not until almost a decade later that its impact began to filter through to policy oriented discussion and controversy. In the process, the doctrine has undergone a certain popularisation and vulgarisation so that its original rigour has often been lost in more popular discussion. However, it is important to note that it is the original and precise Muthian definition which has been taken up by the leading exponents of rational expectations theory, especially in the seminal papers of Lucas and Sargent, and which has generated such major and profound implications for economic analysis and policy. To quote directly from Muth's seminal paper:

> Expectations since they are informed predictions of future events are essentially the same as the predictions of the relevant economic theory... expectations of firms (or more generally the subjective probability distribution of outcomes) tend to be distributed for the same information set, about the prediction of the theory (or the 'objective' probability distribution of outcomes)....

In other words, the rational agent will obtain information about the 'objective' probability distribution of outcomes associated with a particular policy action and analysed with reference to the relevant economic theory, and he will use this information to generate expectations concerning the variable which interests him. Assuming he uses this information efficiently, his prediction or expectations will be identical to the mean value of the distribution of possible outcomes generated by the relevant theory. In the case of an agent concerned with the future price level, for example, this implies that the expected price is in fact an unbiased predictor of the actual price. That is to say, the price anticipated by economic agents is given by the mathematical expectation of the price derived from the formal model analysis (which is assumed to be the correct model for the economy), in conjunction with the available information, including policy announcements by the authorities. Moreover, any subsequent forecast error between the actual price which prevails and the anticipated price is serially uncorrelated with a mean expectation of zero, and is also held to be independent of the anticipated price. What this implies is that when anticipated and actual prices are compared using time series data, deviations between the two are completely randomly distributed around the value zero (where anticipated prices and actual prices coincide). Rational expectations also implies that the expected variation around the mean is equal to the actual variance. It is important to note what the statement does not assert. Predictions (expectations) are not perfect since available information will be incomplete and it does not imply that all agents will possess the same expectation. Nor is it necessary for economic agents to know the true model of the economy. All that is required is for them to form their expectations in the aggregate, *as if* they did know it.

One principal empirical difficulty, raised by the statement, is that people, when questioned, do not appear to form expectations in the context of a formal model of the economy. Nor do they, for the most part, admit to knowing the correct model of the economy. This generates the conclusion that the rational expectations thesis requires economic agents to act in the light of a model they hold subconsciously—a conclusion which many critics find implausible.

It is the strict rigorous version of the rational expectations thesis that has generated conclusions which appear counterfactual. For example, it leads to the proposition that business cycles should consist of random fluctuations in production and employment rather than the observed cycle which exhibits depressed levels of output and employment lasting several years. Other arguments, such as wage and price rigidities or adjustment costs, are then invoked to reconcile the conclusions of the theory with the observed facts of the real world.

Whilst it is the strong Muthian version of the theory which has dominated academic discussion and generated the major implications and policy conclusions, other weaker statements of rational expectations formation have influenced popular debate. At one extreme, for example, the statement is taken to imply no more than that economic agents will form expectations optimally by taking all available information into consideration where 'availability' is defined with respect to cost. Such a statement amounts to little more than the belief that economic agents are utility maximisers. At a somewhat stronger level, as we have already argued, rational expectations formation amounts to an assertion that economic agents will learn to eliminate *systematic* expectational error, and this version carries far greater implications for the conduct of macro-economic policy.

The weaker forms of the rational expectations hypothesis, whilst less demanding intellectually and more acceptable intuitively as a basis of human behaviour, suffer the drawback of comparative vagueness. They do not, for example, indicate clearly the discrepencies which will arise between expectations formed in this manner and the predictions that would be obtained by the correct economic theory. It is important that these differing versions of rational expectations philosophy be kept in mind because in arguing the merits and demerits of the thesis it is not always clear, at least in popular discussion, which version is being discussed at any given moment in time.

6 Rational Expectations, the Natural Rate Hypothesis and the Business Cycle

When dealing with adaptive expectations we paid particular attention to the natural rate hypothesis, summarised in the concept of a long-term vertical Phillips Curve, Deviations from the natural rate, permitting an element of trade-off for the policy making authorities, were shown to derive from the failure upon the part of labour to foresee correctly future inflation rates. Without such failure, output and employment levels would remain invariant over time.

Now this failure can derive from two distinct sources. On the one hand, economic agents may form their expectations naively, i.e., in a non-rational manner. Alternatively, expectational errors may arise by misperception by individuals of the values taken by current economic variables. Such misperception can occur owing to the lack of adequate information or because the cost of acquiring and processing such information is too high. In the former case, that of non-rational expectations formulation, government monetary and fiscal policies can affect output and employment levels if they generate expectations mistakes upon the part of economic agents with regard to future inflation rates. If we postulate rational expectations behaviour, however, the ability of the authorities to generate expectational errors is decidedly curtailed. Indeed, the ability of the authorities to generate *systematic* expectational errors is eliminated.

Since a sensible countercyclical macro-economic policy will follow certain specific rules, determining, for example, how monetary and fiscal changes will respond to certain economic indicators (such as unemployment rates), such policy measures will themselves become systematic and will become predictable. That is to say, economic indicators or observed values of economic variables in the past period will correctly condition the expectation of current values of *policy* variables, providing the policy making authorities pursue a logical stabilisation policy. If this is the case, logical stabilisation policies will become perfectly anticipated by all economic agents; future inflation rates will be correctly judged; individuals will immediately adjust their behavioural pattern in making new contracts, etc.; and the authorities will relinquish any power to influence *systematically* expectational error. What is implied in this statement is simply that if the macro-authorities cannot generate *systematic* expectational error, they likewise cannot exert any *systematic* influence upon employment levels and output. In short, the distinction between the negatively sloped short-run Phillips Curve and the vertically sloped long-run Phillips Curve is eliminated.

This startling conclusion which emerged from the rational expectations literature (Sargent and Wallace 1975) has understandably been given great prominence. It has frequently been invoked to demonstrate how rational expectations *could* frustrate contra-cyclical stabilisation policies and thus deny any meaningful role to the macro-authorities. It is accordingly important to emphasise that the Sargent/Wallace model was but a special case and was not intended to demonstrate that rational expectations philosophy implies policy neutrality as a general phenomenon. Nonetheless, it emphasises the difficulties associated with stabilisation policy and, whilst a special case, it is perhaps indicative of the general spirit which pervades the rational expectations literature.

This must not be taken to imply that policy makers have no influence upon the performance of the macro-economy. If macro-economic policy were essentially random and uncorrelated with past observed economic variables—that is to say, if macro-policy formation were essentially erratic and noncountercyclical in character—then it would have the ability to generate expectational errors upon the part of individual economic agents and thus impinge upon output and employment decisions. But in this event, such errors would be purely random and totally uncorrelated with the values of relevant past economic variables. Needless to say, expectational errors induced in this manner are hardly likely to be conducive to the attainment of macro-economic target goals.

The foregoing, of course, does not rule out the possibility that expectational errors may occur owing to the lack of adequate information possessed by individual economic agents and it may indeed be the case that the macro-authorities may be able to exploit their superior access to the relevant data banks. Moreover, the foregoing presumes economic agents can react speedily to change existing contracts presupposing a good deal of price flexibility. Again, if price flexibility does not prevail to this extent, the government may possess a certain limited ability over the contractual period to influence real magnitudes. The implications of economic agents being unable to exploit their information sets owing to contractual obligations has been developed principally by Fischer (1977) and Phelps and Taylor (1977) and further emphasises the 'special case' feature of the Sargent/Wallace result. Moreover, recent research by Minford and Peel (1981) points to cases where opportunities for stabilisation policy exist even in the absence of contractual constraints and informational differences. Nonetheless, the policy ineffectiveness proposition has been influential in the evolution of economic thought concerning interventionist policy generally, and it is perhaps instructive to examine its relationship with monetarism and supply-side economics.

In the early days of the Keynesian optimism concerning the ability of the authorities to regulate demand so as to generate and maintain full employment income, fiscal policy was given pride of place. Changes in government spending or taxation would, via their associated multiplier impacts, perform the essential services required by demand management. The financial or budgetary consequences could conveniently be ignored. The rise of monetarism was, in large measure, a reaction to this rather *simpliste* Keynesian oriented fiscal approach. Critics, such as Milton Friedman (1969), pointed to the budgetary or financial implications of such policies. The latter would generate monetary or interest rate changes (in turn encompassing wealth effects) which could, in certain conditions, negate or 'crowd out' the intended fiscal impact. The economics of the budget constraint sought to play down the importance of purely fiscal changes and instead emphasised the importance of the accommodating monetary changes in influencing real variables in the short run. However, if monetary magnitudes were now dominant, this influence upon real variables would be but short lived. The natural rate hypothesis was invoked to suggest that the long-run adjustment would be to the natural or full employment level of income. The natural rate hypothesis was fundamental to the monetarist conclusion that monetary changes exert essentially nominal impacts over the long term. Hence the conventional wisdom became one in which fiscal policy was impotent unless accompanied by accommodating monetary changes, whilst the latter would have limited short-run impact upon real variables and would ultimately find expression in the long term solely in their impact upon nominal magnitudes.

The rational expectations hypothesis may now be considered as a logical extension of this line of theorising. By denying *any* possibility of the macro-economic authorities being able to influence *systematically* output and employment levels by *macro-economic* countercyclical policies, rational expectations philosophy is suggesting that output and employment be left to seek out their own natural levels. Indeed, if monetary and fiscal policy cannot *systematically* influence output and employment away from their natural levels even in the short run, then the policy conclusions to be drawn are clear enough, namely;

1   Macro-economic policy should be geared to minimising random or erratic variations in the variables subject to control by the authorities. In this way, random expectational errors which cause the economy to diverge from its natural full employment growth path would be minimised. This suggests possibly fixed

rules such as, for example, the idea that monetary growth should proceed at a constant pace in line with the potential growth path of the economy.

2   If real magnitudes cannot be influenced by sensible macro-economic policies, it would suggest that such policies be directed to the control of the nominal magnitudes which they can influence. Once again, if inflation could be eliminated, or alternatively if its rate could be stabilised, this would be conducive to expectational error upon the part of economic agents being minimised and thus deviations from the natural full employment growth path would likewise be minimised.

The relationship between rational expectations and supply side economics should now be apparent. In particular, and the importance of this point must be emphasised, rational expectations philosophy does not claim that government policies cannot exert favourable impact upon output and employment levels. Rather, its assertion is that this cannot be achieved by *macro-economic* policies designed to raise the level of aggregate demand. However, there may exist suitable *micro-economic* policies able to influence favourably the natural rate of employment. This distinction can best be illustrated by reference to Figure 6.1, where we display the aggregate demand schedule AD^1 in conjunction with the vertical aggregate supply schedule AS^1. The price output combination is accordingly given as P_1Q_1 where Q_1 refers to the natural level of output or employment. Now let us assume an increase in the level of aggregate demand to AD^2. Belief in the invariance of the aggregate supply response means that the entire impact of the demand stimulus will be dissipated in price rises to P_2. There will be no impact, even in the short run, upon output and employment. We are in a world of the strict quantity theory where nominal magnitudes respond to every nominal change but real variables remain invariant. Suppose, however, that the government can influence the *position* of the vertical aggregate supply schedule by the appropriate supply side strategies—that is, by inducing an outward shift of the vertical curve. Such a situation is shown by the dotted curve AS^2 implying larger real

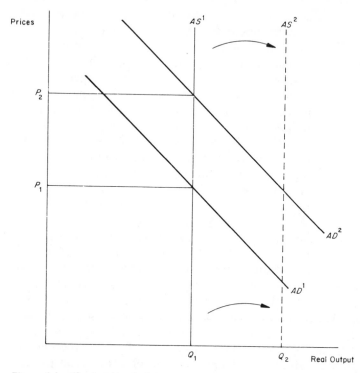

Figure 6.1. Altering Natural Output Levels by Supply Side Strategies

output and lower prices. How can such a favourable shift be
achieved? According to supply side advocates, the answer lies
in the adoption of the relevant micro-economic policies. The
level of unemployment benefits, the existence of minimum
wage laws and so forth may adversely influence the natural
employment level. Equally, tax incentives, or privatisation
have been advocated as a means of stimulating work effort and
efficiency and thus of raising natural output and employment
levels—with, of course, favourable impact upon price levels.
Thus, whilst the rational expectations hypothesis dismisses
countercyclical macro-economic policy as an irrelevancy in the
search for improved output and employment levels, the school
of supply side economics provides, in their view, the only
workable alternative.

The foregoing strongly suggests that the economy will

achieve its natural levels of output and employment and that the macro-authorities will be powerless to generate systematic deviations from such levels. The questions which are immediately raised are, first, why, given these assertions, the business cycle should occur at all and, secondly, why, when fluctuations from natural levels occur, they should persist for so long?

The answer to the first question relies upon expectational error. Expectations may be proved wrong owing to extraneous random shocks or events which, like war or crop failure, could not reasonably have been anticipated at the time expectations were formulated. A theory of the business cycle which depends upon random shock is, of course, very Keynesian in spirit. However, Keynesians differ from rational expectations theorists in believing that given some initial disturbance the economy will not readily adjust back towards the full employment path; indeed, a good deal of neo-Keynesian economics is concerned with the forces which will magnify any divergence from equilibrium and thus will justify active interventionist policies so as to correct and offset such destabilising consequences.

Whilst admitting that autonomous disturbances such as those mentioned above can cause output and employment fluctuation, rational expectations theorists point to another source of disturbance, namely erratic and unpredictable action upon the part of the monetary authorities. Such actions lead to mis-specification on the part of individual economic agents which can then cause fluctuations in real output and employment. Essentially these mis-specifications arise from the absence of perfect information and the costs associated with acquiring and processing information adequately. The lack of adequate information then generates misperceptions concerning *relative* prices and it is these misperceptions which then generate cyclical movements. Nonetheless, such misperceptions will be eliminated over time and the economy will eventually adjust back to the equilibrium path without interventionist policies. Indeed, interventionist policies may do no more than exacerbate the maladjustment by giving rise to further mis-specification. In order to develop this analysis more fully it is necessary to examine in slightly more detail the micro-economic structure upon which rational expectations theory and the neo-classical macro-economics is based.

The Walrasian general equilibrium approach to price theory postulates that the economy consists of a set of highly interdependent markets. A change in the supply or demand conditions occurring in any one market will, by generating income changes for the factors of production involved, exert feedback effects on alternative markets which, in turn, will generate feedback effects upon the market initiating the change. The Walrasian theory thus stands in sharp contrast to the more pragmatic Marshallian approach which focusses upon individual markets in isolation under the assumption of *ceteris paribus*. The Walrasian theory is thus stated in terms of a series of simultaneous supply and demand equations describing all markets throughout the economy. The intriguing question then raised is whether a solution to this complex set of equations will exist. In order to pursue this question it is assumed that all markets clear; indeed, no exchange is permitted to take place in any market at prices which do not equate supply and demand. That is to say, the phenomenon of false trading is ruled out. In addition, Walrasian price theory invokes the assumption that all market participants have perfect knowledge and know the values of all prices in all markets before they actually engage in trading activity. Now these assumptions of market clearing and perfect knowledge or foresight are sufficient to guarantee the conclusion that aggregate output is solely supply determined and can never depart from the equilibrium natural or full employment level. For clearly, if all agents know the value of all prices at all points in time, then they also know the value of all relative prices. Thus, for example, suppose an increase occurs in the level of aggregate nominal demand financed by increased money supply, which generates, in accordance with classical micro-economic theory, a proportionate increase in all prices. The economic agent with perfect knowledge will be aware that all relative prices are unchanged. He will perceive that no change has occurred in any real variable, and in particular no change has occurred with respect to his real wage. Accordingly, he has no incentive to modify his supply of labour; employment remains unchanged and so does the volume of output. All that the nominal demand change can do is to alter the level of nominal prices; the money supply change is strictly neutral with respect to all real variables. In such a world, aggregate supply can only change if some fundamental change occurs in the underlying supply conditions. Thus, for example, technological change or innovation may shift the production function upwards for any given labour input; alternatively, in a dynamic context the supply of labour offered at any given wage may alter with population growth and so forth. Nonetheless, the output level remains impervious to any demand stimuli.

The rational expectations thesis departs from the classical equilibrium framework in one very important respect. It does not assume that all economic agents possess perfect knowledge of all market conditions. This is another way of saying that information is not freely available at zero cost for if it were utility maximising agents would always equip themselves with perfect knowledge. Once it is conceded that information is costly to acquire and process, individual agents may get distorted impressions of true relative prices and price changes. They may not, for example, be fully aware of how changes in the composition of demand generated by changing tastes alter relative prices. They may not enter all markets with the same frequency and, therefore, their knowledge of the less frequented markets may be subject to degenerative decay. One does not, normally speaking, possess the same knowledge of the housing market as one does of the beer market since one's contact with the former is relatively infrequent whilst the latter relatively continuous. Moreover, there will be a time dimension to one's learning process concerning price changes. It is reasonable to assume, for example, that an economic agent will be immediately aware of a change in his nominal rate of pay (or perhaps in the rate of income taxation) which determines his *nominal* take-home pay, whereas he may need time to appreciate how other prices in more distant markets (less frequented markets) have also changed. Thus a distortion may be introduced into his perception of relative prices which may lead him to believe a change has occurred in his real wage and induce him to alter his supply of work effort. The economic agent's mis-specification arises from the absence of complete and costless information; it does not arise from money illusion, it should be noted, and his response is perfectly consistent with rational maximising behaviour.

Let us illustrate this argument in more detail by assuming that the government causes an unanticipated increase in the money supply thus raising the level of aggregate demand. Let us continue to assume that all markets clear, implying that prices are perfectly flexible, but let us also assume that economic agents have imperfect information concerning prices prevailing in markets other than the one in which they trade. *Ceteris paribus,* the increase in nominal monetary demand will raise all prices equiproportionately. However, a seller finding an unexpectedly high price prevailing in *his* market may conclude that *relative* prices have changed in his favour. He may thus be induced to increase his output, unaware that his input costs have also risen, or, if he is a seller of labour services, to increase his supply of work effort, unaware of the increased price of consumption goods. Initially, therefore, there may be real output and employment effects in consequence of the money supply change. Precisely similar reasoning applies to a decrease in nominal aggregate demand occasioned by an unanticipated decrease in the money supply. Money supply changes are no longer neutral in their impacts. Of course, this process does not last indefinitely; sooner or later economic agents will learn about alternative price changes and thus obtain a truer perception of the change in relative prices; when this learning process is complete the economy will again be restored to its Walrasian full employment equilibrium. How long this process will take is for the moment not the point of issue. Nonetheless, implicit in the rational expectations thesis is the concept that the process of adjustment will not be aided by discretionary interventionist macro-policy measures. Such measures will either be anticipated and thus negated by the self-seeking actions of individual economic agents or else, if they are unanticipated, they are as likely to generate destabilising movements similar to that precipitated by the initial deviation from the Walrasian equilibrium path. Given the combination of market clearing assumptions and the doctrine of rational expectations, any deviation from the Walrasian equilibrium path will be self-correcting. However, the conclusion against interventionist policy is stronger than this. Clearly, in the above illustration the unanticipated increase in the money supply did generate a short-lived increase in real output as well as causing prices to rise. Thus the theory would suggest a positive correlation between output change and money supply growth. However, this is not to postulate that there exists a trade-off of the Phillips Curve variety for the authorities to exploit. This is because the increase in output is attained only because the increase in the money supply was greater than had been anticipated. Over the course of the trade cycle, output will be higher when the money supply is higher than had been expected, i.e., higher than average. But when the business cycle is taken as a whole, it is impossible for the money supply, overall, to be higher than average. Thus there is no reason to assume that total output over the cycle will be greater with activist interventionist policies than without. The positive correlation between money supply growth and output growth does not constitute an argument for Keynesian oriented demand management policies.

However, this explanation of the business cycle—rational expectational behaviour plus misperception—is not without certain conceptual problems, especially when the cyclical disturbance is prolonged over any significant period. As we have previously mentioned, one point in favour of the basic rational expectations hypothesis is that individual economic agents have wide access to inexpensive information services provided by the media, as well as enjoying the benefit of highly sophisticated specialist information services provided by membership of trade unions, trade associations and similar organisations enjoying enormous economies of scale in data collection and processing. Both wholesale and retail price indices are published not only with great frequency but, in addition, are accorded such prominence that it becomes virtually impossible not to acquire this information at zero cost. Again, the misperception argument assumes that a contraction of the nominal money stock, leading to reduced prices, will be perceived by labour as a reduction in its own product price and hence in its own real wage. In this case, labour fails to see that the decline in its own product price is part and parcel of general all round deflation. Consequently, labour wrongly concludes that its real wage has fallen in its own particular activity, relative to real wages elsewhere, and thus is induced to leave the industry and seek employment elsewhere. Unemployment, and the subsequent cutback in output, can then be explained in terms of the time required for the unemployed worker, engaged in job search activity, to perceive that his expected nominal wage is now unrealistic. Such wage search or job search unemployment is perfectly consistent with rational maximising behaviour, but how long is it likely to persist before labour realises the true position? How many visits to a job centre are required before the unemployed worker perceives the wage he can realistically expect to obtain? If individual economic agents possess the learning ability required of them not to be misled by sophisticated yet systematic attempts at countercyclical policy imposed by the macro-authorities, is it really sensible to assume that they will require much time to learn about the true state of the employment market?

Of course, it is true that once made, an output or employment decision cannot be reversed with zero costs. There are genuine costs involved in virtually any employment or output decision. The sinking of additional capital resources into the production of durable consumer goods, such as the motor car, cannot suddenly be scrapped without incurring enormous losses. It may accordingly make better sense to continue with the project, in some form or another, even though it is now realised that the original investment decision was based on incorrect or insufficient information. In a similar vein, if you resign your job in a fit of pique over what you perceive to be a relative decline in your real wage, you cannot expect to be able to reclaim it the next morning after a more sober reappraisal. Thus initial employment and output effects of misperception may continue for a while even though the initial misperception is now corrected. Nonetheless, such considerations are hardly likely to account for the business cycle lasting over a period of years.

The misperception thesis would be far more convincing if there were a significant time lag existing between the decision to sell one's labour services and the decision to buy one's consumption goods. In this event, one might reasonably infer a mistaken impression of the real wage. But in fact, most economic agents are sellers of labour services and active consumers at the same time. For many families the distinction between worker/shopper roles is distinctly blurred. Even in the more traditional family relationships where a dichotomy prevails between breadwinner and provider of household services, does anyone really imagine that the breadwinner will not be speedily and reliably informed when the cost of bread goes up?

In summary, the theory of misperception is a logical and sensible attempt to explain the observed deviations from natural full employment equilibrium levels of output and employment in a manner consistent with utility maximising behaviour. However, as it stands, it seems inadequate to explain the duration of the cycle over a prolonged period of years—especially when, as in the present case, employment below its equilibrium level is predicted to continue well into the future by all the reputable forecasting models. Surely, utility maximising individuals would not require such a prolonged period of time to adjust their expectations downwards in the light of all known information? Suppose, however, that individual agents are prevented from making the required adjustment by the existence of price and wage inflexibility in certain markets. In this case, if we dispense with the market clearing assumption of the new classical macro-economics, the misperception thesis becomes much more credible as an explanation for extended cyclical disturbance. We may still posit maximising behaviour and we may still assume rational expectations, but the combination of misperception together with relative price inflexibility can then be combined to account for the observed fact of the business cycle. The question which then remains—and which rational expectations theorists rightly raise—is why should rational maximising agents combine together to generate wage and price rigidity. It is to this question, *inter alia*, that we now turn.

7 Rational Expectations and Price Flexibility

The preceding chapter has clearly indicated the overriding importance of the question of price flexibility for the implications to be derived from the rational expectations doctrine. Much of the new classical macro-economics, and in particular the policy ineffectiveness proposition, derives from the assumption of an almost unlimited degree of price and wage flexibility which, in turn, implies continuous market clearing activity. In short, many rational expectations theorists appear to maintain a view of the economy which conforms very closely to the Walrasian framework.

This assumption of market clearing behaviour stands in marked contrast to recent interpretations of Keynes. Leijonhufvud (1968) in particular has argued that what Keynes was really attempting to do was to demonstrate that, whilst a market clearing price vector could exist for all markets, the market economy left to its own devices might be incapable of achieving it. In such an event, false trading would occur, especially in the labour market, implying output changes in place of price (wage) changes which, via income effects, may exert destabilising feedback effects upon other markets, moving the economy further and further away from its full employment equilibrium.

In fact, of course, the empirical evidence clearly indicates that different markets indicate substantial differences in the speed of price adjustment of changes in nominal aggregate demand. The response is markedly slower in markets where administered prices prevail or where firms follow 'full cost

73

pricing' policies and thus insulate themselves, at least initially, from changing demand pressures. Such insensitivity, of course, implies at least partial quantity adjustment to nominal demand changes. The theoretical dichotomy is thus matched by an empirical dichotomy, and the issue is further complicated by the lack of any fully articulated theory to account for such diversity and to reconcile the observed dichotomy with conventional maximising postulates of economic theory.

New classical market clearing models gain greatly in elegance and tractability by assuming a one-product economy in which all producers are price takers operating in competitive conditions. It then becomes perfectly logical to analyse such models in terms of efficient auction markets which generate market clearing conditions. Under these conditions, the failure to obtain supply and demand equilibrium (implying false trading) can only be explained in the absence of full information which falsifies one's perception of the true magnitude of aggregate nominal demand. The appeal of such models is further enhanced by the obvious reference to maximising behaviour. Indeed, at one extreme, Barro (1979) has argued that the assumption of market clearing is implied by the assertion that individual economic agents engage in utility maximising behaviour. This follows since the equation of supply and demand implies that all mutually advantageous trading has been exhausted. Alternatively, if supply and demand are not equated, it follows that some mutually advantageous transactions opportunities still remain.

In a market organised along the lines of a Walrasian auction, the assumption of market clearing appears a reasonable one to make. And there is no doubt that certain markets readily lend themselves to such auction trading. When the product is sufficiently standardised and uniform to be homogeneous from the subjective vantage point of the buyer, as in the case of certain financial markets and commodity markets, the potential buyer need not 'inspect' the product at all; he has all the information he needs, obtained most inexpensively, to make a rational decision and he can then enter such a market through the services of a specialist agent or broker. Such markets will, accordingly, tend to be dominated by specialist traders, possessed of considerable stocks of the good in question, and it is reasonable to assume that such markets will operate very closely to the market clearing price.

This conclusion rests upon the fact that in such a market every trader will have the incentive to estimate both what the market clearing price is ultimately going to be and also when such a price is going to occur. If he is possessed of such information he will be able to exploit his knowledge—either by buying or selling—to make abnormal profits. However, the same incentive will be open to all specialist traders; they will have the time and effort and resources to generate and process the required information. Given the existence of competition, and in particular equal potential access to the relevant data, all specialist traders will tend to generate expectations of the market clearing price which coincide within fairly narrow limits. In such conditions, actual prices will invariably be close to market clearing prices. Accordingly, such markets, deemed 'efficient markets', are characterised by flexible prices. Or, to use the term initially invoked by Hicks (1974), they are *flexprice* markets. The behaviour of specialist traders described above is, of course, entirely in keeping with rational expectations formulation. The only difference in their behaviour from that of the 'average' economic agent is that they find it worthwhile to collect and analyse a far greater volume of information. Indeed, the absence of sustained abnormal profits in such specialist markets is often invoked as evidence of rational expectations formation.

It is but a short step to assert that what is undeniably utility maximising behaviour in specialist financial and commodity markets should logically be utility maximising behaviour in any other market—hence the assertion that market clearing is a generalised phenomenon throughout the economy, implying considerable general wage and price flexibility.

However, this is to overlook the fact that many markets do not deal in standardised homogeneous products—the labour market is but one. In such markets, potential buyers wish to inspect (interview) the product personally; they are not willing to leave the market to specialist traders. When products are decidedly heterogeneous, markets tend not to be dominated by specialist traders and in such markets the costs of acquiring information concerning the future market clearing price will tend to be relatively high, whilst the associated benefits may be relatively low. An agent trading in such a market, for example, will often not possess the requisite inventory stock to make a killing if he feels existing prices are too high, and in the case of labour services it is not possible to store the product if one believes existing prices to be too low. Such markets may not exhibit great price flexibility, or their price flexibility may be subject to a considerable time dimension. In terms of the Hicksian dichotomy, such markets are *fixprice* markets.

An alternative way of making this point is in terms of the transaction costs imposed upon the buyers. Auction sales can be applied to certain markets where the size of the transaction is large (a house, work of art, etc.) or where the physical presence of the buyer is not required (stocks, shares, commodity markets, etc.). For other commodities and for small-scale transactions in consumer goods and services, an auction market would impose tremendous costs upon market participants—not least the cost of time and the inconvenience of attending a fixed location at a prescribed time. Price fixing permits goods to be freely available at many locations at times convenient for the purchaser and on known terms which avoid the time consuming auction process. As Gordon (1981) succinctly expresses it: 'The use of a price tag instead of a live trader or auctioneer can also be viewed as a substitution of cheap capital for expensive labor.' It is thus perfectly rational and sensible, and consistent with maximising behaviour, to announce fixed prices and to maintain them over lengthy periods, and there can be no doubt as a matter of empirical fact that many prices remain unchanged even over cyclical periods. It is avoidance of the adjustment costs implied by auction markets which accounts for market non-clearing and which explains why adjustment will occur upon the side of quantity changes as opposed to price.

Alchian (1969) makes much the same point in arguing that stable prices reduce search costs imposed upon consumers. In a vivid example, he cites the possible need for market clearing to require the doubling of restaurant prices on exceptionally busy evenings, compelling patrons to undertake research costs rather than be able to visit the restaurant of their choice. A fixed price which prevails over a reasonable time, and which only alters in line with general cost inflation, may be the optimal strategy designed to attach a customer to a particular source of supply. Indeed, for similar reasons sellers may be quite rationally justified in entering into contractual agreements to supply at a given price over a relatively long period, without departing from assumptions consistent with profit maximising behaviour.

Moreover, there may be many valid reasons why rational maximising agents choose to adopt fixed prices and maintain them even when they are aware that they differ from the market clearing price. Employed workers, for example, perceiving considerable unemployment all around them, may reasonably conclude that the going wage exceeds the market clearing wage. Nonetheless, they will have no incentive to adjust their wage rate downwards as long as they are reasonably confident of maintaining their jobs. Indeed, since orthodox economic theory teaches both that diminishing marginal productivity applies to labour inputs and that real wages are equal to labour's marginal product, it follows that any increase in employment must imply a decrease in the real wage. Accordingly, employed workers with reasonable job security will, unless they are extremely altruistic in their attitudes, have no wish to see the level of unemployment decline under *ceteris paribus* conditions. In part, this may explain the relative lack of concern upon the part of the employed with the plight of the unemployed school-leaver.

Moreover, from the vantage point of sellers of products, a certain degree of fixpricety will be required for rational trading behaviour. A price if set must prevail for long enough to allow potential buyers to become aware of it if it is going to indicate the appropriate signals. There are also significant costs attached to making price changes, not least the cost of informing sales staff and possibly also of changing national advertising schedules.

In the modern economy, most firms are price setters and the prices they set are geared to long-run estimated trends. It will simply not pay them to adjust prices to every short-run change in demand, especially when such changes have not been demonstrated to be permanent. Even when the changed demand condition is expected to be of reasonable permanency, however, a firm may still prefer to leave prices unaltered and let the adjustment fall upon production levels or inventory changes if the indicated price adjustment is relatively small. Given that there are lump-sum costs attached to a price change, which, for the most part will be independent of the extent of the price change, profit maximising strategy may dictate a policy of relatively infrequent price changes with fairly discrete jumps, as opposed to a policy of almost continuous price adjustments of infinitely small amounts. In this scenario, the profit maximising firm establishes the profit maximising price-output combination by reference to the relevant criteria. The price so established is then held fixed until such time as the same criterion justifies a new price which exceeds or falls short of the old one by a given absolute amount. During this interval, which may be considerable, all adjustments will be quantity adjustments and market clearing conditions will not hold.

Further, price rigidity will to a large extent be a consequence of the highly complex and interdependent market economy, being unable to achieve the degree of coordination required by the Walrasian theory. In the latter situation, the existence of the benevolent auctioneer ensures that perfect information exists and that no false trading can ever occur. What happens, however, in the absence of the auctioneer? This is the question to which Leijonhufvud calls attention in his interpretation of Keynes; one implication is that the existence of uncertainty may inhibit the market clearing price adjustments. Suppose, for example, that the government by its fiscal policy brings about a fall in monetary demand. A firm may perceive that in order to leave output and employment unchanged it will have to reduce its price. Moreover, it may also be aware that the price reduction will not affect its profitability providing that prices throughout the economy, including input prices, all fall in proportion to the decline in monetary demand. Suppose this perception is generalised to all firms in the economy. The question still remains, which firm will make the first move? No firm will unilaterally cut its price without the assurance that all other firms will do the same. The same argument, of course, applies to any one trade union. It is partly on account of the uncertainty concerning the response of others to a general demand change that prices reveal rigidity and the weight of adjustment is thrown upon quantity and hence employment changes. In the highly complex modern economy, it is this failure of coordination amongst many diverse competing groups that makes the analogy with specialised financial markets essentially false. It is this lack of coordination which delays the impact of nominal demand changes upon prices and ensures that some impact will be transmitted to real variables.

The preceding argument implies that the firm may not embark upon price changing strategy even when it is aware of the prices required to restore market clearing conditions. However, the firm may also be unaware of what price changes are required. In all likelihood, the firm will perceive a change in the demand conditions confronting its final product before it perceives that similar revised demand conditions pertain to its intermediate and factor inputs. If it acts in this manner, it may falsely translate a uniform change in aggregate demand into a relative demand change for its own product and alter its output decisions accordingly. The consequence is to generate a smaller price response than that required for market equilibrium, and it is this lesser response which guarantees that some part of the nominal demand change will be transmitted to quantity adjustments.

This argument can best be illustrated by reference to the familiar profit maximising monopolist who, for simplicity, is assumed to possess constant marginal costs.[1] In Figure 7.1 the original profit maximising price-output combination is given by $P_1 Q_1$, determined by the intersection of the constant marginal cost curve MC_1, with the marginal revenue curve MR_1 corresponding to the initial demand curve D_1. Let us now assume that government monetary policy leads to demand deflation so that the firm perceives its demand falling to D_2, and its corresponding marginal revenue curve becoming MR_2. Now if the firm falsely assumes that its marginal costs are unaltered, it will adjust to the new output level Q_2 and adjust price to P_2. However, if the decline in the firm's demand curve is but part and parcel of a general deflationary movement, its marginal costs should fall to MC_2—a reduction exactly equal to the decline in the firm's demand for its product. In this event, the indicated price reduction is to P_3 which leaves the firm's

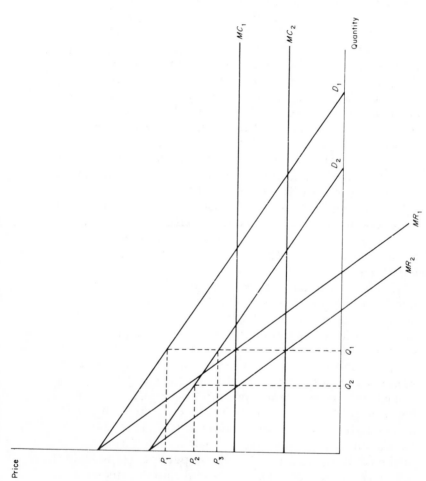

Figure 7.1. Real versus Perceived Demand and Cost Changes

real output level unchanged. This failure upon the part of the firm to perceive equality between demand changes and cost changes emanating from government monetary policy will ensure that some impact is transmitted onto quantity adjustments.[2] But this type of failure is precisely what we might expect since demand changes will be observed first in markets for final goods whereas intermediate goods producers will experience a lagged response.

Again, contractual obligations may limit price flexibility in labour markets and yet be judged perfectly rational by both parties to the wage bargain. Labour for its part may, because of risk aversion, be willing to enter into a relatively long-term contract at a given wage (possibly with some element of index linking) as a form of 'insurance'. On the employer's side, the cost of hiring labour and in particular of replacing experienced workers may be extremely high. In such circumstances, the employer may feel the need to offer inducements to skilled labour in the form of some guarantee of incremental wage increases over a relatively long period. Hence an element of wage rigidity and especially a wage floor may be incorporated into long-term contractual obligations as a logical consequence of optimal behaviour in markets where both employer and employee face significant transactions costs.

Finally, it must be remembered that the labour market differs from other markets in one very important respect, as both Hicks (1974) and Solow (1980) have emphasised. Behaviour in labour markets is conditioned by social conventions, custom, and a conduct of behaviour which is in some sense moral. Unemployed workers seeking employment apply at the going market wage. They do not approach employers and offer themselves in place of an employed worker for £5 or $5 a week less. Nor do employers respond to a situation of general unemployment by sacking their existing work force with a view to replacing it at a lower cost. A sense of what is appropriate and what is fair will prevail, implying that in labour markets false trading may be maintained for indefinite periods. Nor should it be assumed that such behaviour is irrational. As long as such conventions exist and as long as social pressures stemming from some concept of a moral code apply, then it is perfectly rational to determine one's behaviour in the light of them.

What is implied in this analysis is that where markets display comparative price and wage rigidity, in the attempt to minimise transactions costs, monetary changes in the level of aggregate demand can exert real effects. Moreover, these real effects can be relatively long-lasting. In contrast, the rational expectations plus misperception approach, whilst able to offer a logically coherent explanation of why deviations from natural full employment levels of output may occur, does not appear to be able to offer a convincing explanation as to why such deviations should be of such duration as is empirically observed. It is perhaps a reluctance to dispense with the price clearing mechanism of the Walrasian framework, and the implied conflict with optimising behaviour, which has made rational expectations theorists hesitant to accept price inflexibilities. Without this assumption, however, the rational expectations explanation of the business cycle lacks conviction. The need is surely for a firmer theoretical foundation of the observed phenomenon of wage and price inflexibility.

NOTES

1   The argument here follows Gordon (1981).
2   It will be appreciated that the argument here does not rely upon a zero perception of marginal cost changes as implied in our diagramatic presentation. As long as the firm perceives its cost reduction to be less than its demand reduction, its price adjustment will fall short of that required and some impact will be transmitted to the real sector.

8 Rational Expectations and Macro-Econometrics

An econometric model consists of a series of simultaneous equations describing the behaviour of the components of the model. These include the *endogenous* variables which are determined by the workings of the model itself. For example, in a national income model we might expect consumption to be endogenous upon income — being dependent upon the ultimate value of national income. Secondly, there are exogenous variables which exert an influence upon the model's outcome but are strictly independent of the model itself. We may distinguish between exogenous variables, such as the rate of taxation and the level of government expenditure, which we assume are subject to control by the authorities, and 'pure' exogenous variables, for example, the level of export demand, which are outside the control of the government.[1] Finally, we will include aleatory or random elements (essentially unpredictable shocks) which affect the outcome of the model analysis. Normally, the latter are included in order to complete the model and allow for errors of observation, influences omitted, and mis-specification, etc., but conventionally are assumed to be serially uncorrelated with other variables and possessed of an expected mean value of zero. Of course, the choice of the relevant variables included in the model is suggested by economic theory. Thus, in the above example, there is a considerable body of economic theory postulating a link between consumption and income although there may exist considerable disagreement upon the appropriate definition of income. One purpose of econometric model building is to resolve these issues of definition by finding the most appropriate definitions which best explain the alleged relationship. Thus, for example, if we posit that consumption is geared to income, we might find a better relationship is obtained (a better fit) if we relate consumption to disposable income.

Essentially, the purpose of economic modelling is to provide an explanation of how the economy behaves. That is to say, we are seeking a set of *structural* equations which explain the nature of the dependence of the endogenous variables. When we say an equation is structural, we mean it describes the behaviour of some recognisable sector of the economy, as for example, how consumers respond to a change in income. The usefulness of such a structural equation will depend upon reasonable stability characterising the values of the parameters. Normally, time series data are invoked to obtain estimates of the parameters or coefficients describing these relationships. For example, if we posit that consumption depends upon disposable income such that

$$C = a + bY$$

where C and Y represent consumption and disposable income respectively, b is the marginal propensity to consume and a the amount consumed at zero income, then by looking at the past relationship between C and Y we can derive estimates of the values taken by a and b. The precise statistical techniques need not concern us here; essentially what is involved is a sophisticated form of extrapolation from the past record. However, what is important is that once the values of these coefficients are obtained they are assumed to be invariant or, if not, certainly extremely stable. This assumption then permits us to forecast or predict how consumption will respond to a change in disposable income from whatever cause, and it is then but a short step to the claim that we can predict how consumption will respond to government policy (say tax policy) designed to change the level of disposable income.

Actual models of the modern economy are often extremely complex, involving, in some cases, literally hundreds of simultaneous equations. Nonetheless, the basic principle remains the same, and rests upon the tacit assumption that the structural parameters underlying the model are not themselves influenced by policy measures initiated by government agencies. This is precisely the issue raised by rational expectations theory, namely that some of the structural parameters will change, and change significantly in response to government policy measures. Thus the question raised by the rational expectations school falls into two parts; first, which structural parameters alter in response to government policy measures and, secondly, in the case of those parameters which do alter, how is this change to be modelled? Unless these questions can be answered adequately, formal econometric models of the economy will be futile in their attempt to predict the outcome of macro-economic policy intervention on the progress of the economy.

The Keynesian revolution, and more especially the translation of the Keynesian system into the Hicksian simultaneous equation framework, provided tremendous incentive to model building and econometric estimation procedures. By the 1960s, fairly sophisticated econometric models existed which were both consistent with the past historical record and performed *short-term* forecasting exercises, including the outcome of government policies, relatively well. However, once we depart from short-term forecasting exercises, the record of the major econometric models is increasingly called into question. In particular, Keynesian oriented models which assume an inflation/employment trade-off as implied by a stable Phillips' relation were shown to be widely incorrect in the inflationary trauma which characterised the 1970s. It is now fairly well agreed that the fundamental weakness of Keynesian-type models was that they were constructed on inadequate microeconomic foundations and paid insufficient attention to utility maximising behaviour upon the part of economic agents participating in the market economy, especially in the labour market. Accordingly, structural parameters which were assumed constant proved in the event to be decidedly unstable and gave rise to extremely disappointing forecasts of economic activity and the effects of discretionary fiscal policy. Keynesian economists have accepted many of these criticisms and have attempted to base their formal models on more sophisticated specifications of behaviour, paying greater attention to the implications of micro-economic maximising strategy. Rational expectations theorists, however, dismiss as futile any econometric modelling which does not formally incorporate rational expectations formation, since the latter implies structural parameters change in response to interventionist macroeconomic policy. There are, however, as the reader might intuitively suspect, considerable difficulties in modelling rational expectations. In what follows, we will attempt to indicate what these difficulties involve and how rational expectations models have tried to overcome them.

One difficulty in econometric model building turns upon the question of identification, by which we mean whether it is possible in principle, with unlimited data, to estimate all the relevant parameters of the model. An equation is said to be identified if all its parameters are identified, and a model is said to be identified if all its equations are identified. Unfortunately, in some cases identification may be extremely difficult or even impossible and arguably problems of identification are more difficult in rational expectations models.

In elementary econometrics, it is a commonplace to demonstrate that structural parameters will not be identified merely by examination of the available data. Some formal economic theory will be required to delineate the relationships. An illustrative example of this problem is provided by Begg (1982b). Suppose wealth is also a determinant of consumption in addition to income. Then it may be possible to determine the relationship between consumption and wealth by examining the historical record of consumption and wealth changes. But assume that wealth also enters as a determinant of investment spending. An increase in wealth will now exert two distinct effects: it will raise consumption directly but also it will stimulate investment, income growth and hence induce indirect increases in consumption spending, working through the marginal propensity to consume. Accordingly, it becomes considerably more difficult to determine the precise parameter values describing the relationship between consumption and wealth merely by examination of the historical record.

This type of difficulty is arguably of more importance in rational expectations modelling because the observed data may encompass *dual* influences of a change in some exogenous variable. On the one hand, they may reflect a lagged response of an endogenous variable to the exogenous change, but also they may encompass a rational expectations element in that former values of the exogenous variables will condition current values which, in turn, may impinge upon the rational expectation of the endogenous variable under consideration. To illustrate, suppose a tax change occurring at time $t - 1$ has a direct effect upon consumption at time t working through disposable income at time t. In addition, however, the tax change occurring at time $t - 1$ may influence the tax rate prevailing in time t and enter into the expectation of disposable income prevailing in time t which also impinges upon consumption outlays. In such cases, it becomes extremely difficult to determine the precise parameters pertaining to the dual influence of the lagged exogenous variable.

A further difficulty arises with rational expectations models. Such models explicitly distinguish between the effects of unanticipated changes in policy variables from the effects of such changes which are anticipated. How does the econometric model decide between changes which are anticipated and those which are not? The only way that it is possible to answer this question is to generate a forecast of what, let us say, monetary supply change would be, given some consistent monetary policy. Thus, for example, let us assume that the Federal Reserve System will raise the money supply in the current period in response to a rise in the unemployment rate in the preceding period.[2] Such an assumption permits us to construct *ex post* a series of the anticipated movement in the money supply. Deviations of the actual observed monetary change from this trend then provide the series of unanticipated monetary growth. Such findings are then utilised to support the proposition that only unanticipated monetary changes exert any real effects upon real variables whereas anticipated changes do not. A number of difficulties follow. First, how robust are such results to an alternative specification of the reaction of the authorities in contemplating money supply changes? One could construct a different type of money supply reaction geared, say, to interest rate changes or movements in the external exchange rate. In recent years, in particular, there is evidence that monetary authorities consistently sought goals other than just employment goals.

Another logical difficulty to this procedure has been raised by Weintraub (1980). He argues that the use of the unemployment rate to separate the money supply into anticipated and unanticipated components is inappropriate unless the Federal authorities are behaving in an irrational way or do not know how the economy works. The reason is that if expectations are formed rationally, the Federal Reserve must know that systematic changes in monetary growth to unemployment changes will have no effect other than upon the price level. Hence it will have no incentive to make systematic monetary changes. In a rational world, the public will come to know this and will accordingly not place any reliance upon the observed relationship between lagged unemployment and monetary growth figures. The argument here is that the Federal Reserve authorities should be at least as rational as the public, and if this is the case then their respective behaviour can best be analysed as a kind of two-person game with the Federal Reserve System possibly possessing informational advantages. In the scenario depicted, however, countercyclical policy is assumed to operate in a decidedly irrational manner.

There are many other points which could be raised concerning the econometric methodology involved in rational expectations modelling.[3] For a survey of the major issues the reader is referred to Mishkin (1983). For present purposes, however, it is perhaps more instructive to consider some of the issues raised by the empirical findings.

First of all, consider highly organised financial markets where transactions costs are relatively minimal, buying and selling relatively continuous and where one would expect the degree of price flexibility to be extremely high indicating market clearing conditions. Here, one assumes that there is great incentive to collect and process information and that the price of financial assets will fully reflect all the available information. If expectations are formed rationally, opportunities of abnormal profits will be speedily eliminated, whereas if this is not the case and agents participating in the market are making systematic errors then the opportunities for profit making will be considerable. There can be no doubt that the empirical findings indicate a broad consensus of opinion that such markets do indeed behave rationally. The general idea, is to test whether the potential for profit making activity exists through arbitrage activity using information contained in past prices. Negative conclusions offer support to the rational expectations thesis. Recently an interesting paper by Daly and Mayor (1983) has applied a similar approach to a real asset market — the market for used cars in the light of OPEC oil price rises in 1973 and 1979. Their findings, namely that the price of fuel-efficient second-hand cars rose relative to the price of fuel-inefficient second-hand cars, suggest that economic agents process information relatively efficiently, in keeping with the general tenor of the rational expectations philosophy.

Further evidence giving general support to the basic ideas underlying rational expectations philosophy may be culled from observations concerning the relationship between money supply changes and changes in nominal interest rates. In Keynesian oriented models, with relatively stable parameters, an increase in monetary growth promotes (normally) a reduction in interest rates, stimulating both investment spending directly and consumption spending indirectly via induced wealth effect changes. This is the reason why Keynesian models attach particular attention to the interest rate consequence of monetary change. However, opposing this general tendency, and more in keeping with the rational expectations outlook, is the fact that monetary growth will raise expectations of future inflation which, in turn, may promote a raising of nominal interest rates. (Recall our parable of Chapter 1.) Simple evidence culled from regressing interest rate changes against money stock changes is far from conclusive (indeed, one may dispute the direction of causation) but in general does not support the Keynesian view. More importantly, rational expectations models which distinguish between anticipated and unanticipated changes in the money supply and which would suggest that unanticipated monetary changes would affect interest rates are not supported by the empirical findings. This would imply that even unanticipated monetary changes can be rapidly translated into inflation expectations. However, this is not to assert that all adjustments need be complete and there may still be impacts upon *real* rates of interest.

By far the most controversial aspect of the empirical findings turns upon the issue of whether anticipated changes in aggregate demand policy will exert any real effect upon output and employment. We have already indicated some of the difficulties associated with the empirical research in this area, in particular with the division of policy into anticipated and unanticipated components. Rational expectations theory would suggest following the Sargent/Wallace model that systematic stabilisation policy would be entirely ineffective given the assumptions of market clearing behaviour and equal access to information upon the part of the government and private sector. In contrast, if market clearing does not hold, or if governmental agencies have superior information sources, then stabilisation policies may exert real impacts upon output and employment even under rational expectations behaviour. Empirically, the issue is complicated by the fact that variations in the level of employment may arise from variations in the natural rate of employment, which themselves may stem from changes in essentially micro-economic policies, in marginal tax rates, unemployment benefits and so forth. Early studies, particularly the seminal papers by Barro (1977, 1978), provided support for the viewpoint that anticipated monetary policy produced no real effects. However, later studies, particularly Mishkin (1982), have questioned these results and have argued that anticipated policies do have real effects and, moreover, exert effects equal in their significance to effects exerted by unanticipated changes—in direct conflict with the policy ineffectiveness proposition of the rational expectations school. Significant in this difference of finding is the lag structure incorporated into the formal models; the longer the lag of output and employment upon policy change, the weaker the evidence in favour of policy ineffectiveness. Finally, it may be noted that many commentators distinguish between the effectiveness of monetary and fiscal policy change. Although some monetarist oriented rational expectations theorists are willing to translate fiscal policy changes into monetary changes via the medium of the budget constraint, and then work entirely within the confines of the monetary change, others are willing to concede that fiscal policy changes will exert real effects even when anticipated or pre-announced. Tax changes, for example, in contrast to purely monetary changes, may change relative prices and thus change the composition of output. Investment tax credits, for example, will surely stimulate more investment and hence may alter the long-term potential supply path of the economy.

At the present time, the controversies upon these issues continue without definite resolution. Nor, given the complexities of the many issues raised is it likely that they will be resolved and a consensus prevail within the foreseeable future. However, where agreement undoubtedly already prevails is on the importance of rational expectations for both economic theory and empirical research. It has changed the way we view the modern interdependent macro-economy and has been of fundamental importance in the design of new empirical research programmes.

NOTES

1 Strictly speaking, of course, the government will be able to exert some influence upon export demand. Its own domestic economic policy will provoke some foreign repercussion with feedback effects upon the demand for exports. But this element of control will be minimal compared to its authority over monetary and fiscal changes.
2 This is the assumption posited in Barro's seminal paper (1977b).
3 One major difficulty in the empirical testing of a rational expectations model derives from the fact that it is a *dual* hypothesis which is subject to scrutiny. On the one hand, there is the need to test for the appropriate expectations mechanism, but on the other, there is an economic model describing the presumed structure of the economy. Failure to verify derived equations by reference to the data need not repudiate the expectations mechanism — it may spring from the invocation of the wrong model. On the other hand, of course, the model may be correct and the expectations assumption false. Worse still, both the model and the expectations mechanism may be defective.

9 Rational Expectations and the Role of Fiscal Policy

The policy implications stemming from the rational expectations doctrine have been concerned primarily with monetary changes and culminate in the conclusion that *anticipated* changes in the money stock can exert no real effects upon output and employment. On occasions, this emphasis has been carried over to the sphere of fiscal policy. Fiscal changes, it is argued, are important only insofar as they influence the money stock; accordingly, anticipated fiscal policy will be as impotent in its effects as anticipated monetary policy. This extreme monetarist interpretation of fiscal policy emphasises the role of the budget constraint and claims that any fiscal action has financial implications; an increase in the budget deficit, for example, must be financed by an increase in the high powered money supply, an increase in the volume of bond holding or some combination of the two. In the United Kingdom, in particular, it has been argued that the size of the budget deficit, or more correctly the size of the Public Sector Borrowing Requirement (PSBR), is the principal determinant of the change in the money supply, even when the deficit is financed by additional bond holding.[1]

However, even if we were to accept this extreme monetarist interpretation of fiscal policy change it does not imply that fiscal changes *per se* will have no real effects. Tax rate changes, for example, are capable of altering relative prices—including the price of leisure. Again, the introduction of an investment tax credit scheme, for example, available for a limited period, is certainly likely to stimulate investment during that period even if it had been previously anticipated. This ability to influence relative prices, an ability generally denied to money supply change, renders fiscal policy measures potentially more effective. Indeed, it is on account of this potency that many supply siders, often sympathetic to the rational expectations doctrine, have advocated tax changes as a means of favourably altering natural rates of employment and output. Reductions in the marginal rate of income taxation are held to be conducive to work effort, saving and risk taking, whilst reductions in certain transfer payments, such as unemployment benefits and similar welfare benefits, are also claimed to provide incentives for employment and affect the natural rate of output favourably. The composition of the tax mix, especially its allocation between direct and indirect taxes, is yet another example of a fiscal instrument able, it is alleged, to influence natural employment levels. The arguments here pertain to effecting a desirable outward shift of the vertical aggregate supply function as previously depicted in Figure 6.1.

Accordingly, the ineffectiveness of policy proposition, as applied to fiscal policy, is to be understood to refer to the ineffectiveness of attempts at expansionary fiscal policy reflected in an enlarged size of the government deficit. Increases in government spending, or decreases in taxation, will be quickly translated into inflationary expectations by rational expectations agents who will then modify their behaviour accordingly. However, it does not necessarily follow that there will be no real impact, especially in the short term. In what follows we will review the arguments concerning the ability of fiscal change to influence consumption outlays. Surprisingly, we conclude that inflationary expectations may enhance fiscal policy effectiveness.

The Keynesian consumption function relates present consumption to current disposable income—or in more sophisticated treatments to a combination of current and immediately preceding disposable income streams. Several important implications immediately arise for fiscal policy. Changes in the rate of taxation, for example, have an immediate effect upon disposable income and hence upon the level of current consumption outlays. Changes in the level of consumption generate multiplier impacts throughout the rest of the economy thus magnifying the initial impact. Changes in taxation, therefore, are seen as a principal means, in addition to changes in government expenditure, of changing the *flow* of expenditures throughout the economy and hence of pursuing stabilisation policies. Belief that the marginal propensity to consume was both relatively high and relatively stable provided the authorities with the means to 'fine tune' the economy so as to maintain reasonably full employment levels of output.

The difficulty with such a formulation, however, is that it suggests a more volatile pattern of consumption behaviour than appears borne out in practice. Consumption appears to be more stable than fluctuations in disposable income would suggest.[2] Partly in response to this objection, several alternative hypotheses of consumer behaviour have emerged. Amongst the better known are the permanent income hypothesis of consumption associated with the name of Milton Friedman (1957) and the life cycle hypothesis of consumption associated in particular with the names of Ando and Modigliani (1963).[3] Essentially, these statements rest upon the assumption of maximising utility strategy upon the part of economic agents and postulate that diminishing marginal utility applies to consumption. It is then a comparatively simple matter to demonstrate that utility will be maximised over time by averaging out consumption as opposed to consuming a lot in periods of high income and economising in periods of relatively low income.

Both the permanent income and the essentially similar life cycle hypothesis involve the notion that consumers plan their consumption behaviour over a relatively long period. Sensible planning thus requires an estimate of what future income levels are expected to be over the same period. Given such expectations, it is then possible to plan for positive savings in periods of relatively high incomes and negative savings during periods of relatively low incomes in order to achieve the utility maximising constant level of consumption spending. The fundamental idea can be summarised in the simple life cycle model of Figure 9.1. Let the income stream be equal to Y over the years of working life ON. Then lifetime income is accordingly YN. If one's expected lifetime is OL years then the optimal consumption pattern is given by $YN/OL = \bar{C}$ with maximum asset holdings occurring at time N. This diagram follows that of Modigliani (1966) and is admittedly extremely simple. Nonetheless, it conveys the essential idea and can be readily modified to take account of inherited wealth, the desire to bequeath wealth, and the possibility of unequal real income streams over one's working life.

The fiscal implications of the permanent income or life cycle theories are considerable. In brief, they minimise the role of fiscal policy or, if that is perhaps an overstatement, they minimise the role of compensatory *tax* changes. Tax changes will impinge upon consumption spending only to the extent that they impinge upon permanent income streams. Obviously, a tax change will have a much smaller impact upon permanent income than upon current income—especially when the tax change is expected to be of short duration.[4] Accordingly, it will exert a much weaker macro-economic impact than implied in the simple Keynesian theory. Indeed, under certain extreme assumptions, in particular the assumption that future government expenditures are not affected by the tax change, it may be demonstrated that a tax change will have zero impact upon permanent income levels (Barro, 1974). A tax cut, for example, will generate the expectation of future tax rate increases, leaving the expectation of permanent income unaltered over the relevant time horizon.

The empirical findings do indicate that consumption responds to change in current income. If the response is not as great as implied by the more naive Keynesian models, it is nonetheless greater than that implied by permanent income/life cycle theory. The discrepancy is usually explained in terms of market imperfections. For example, economic participants cannot always enter the capital market to borrow and lend at will in order to remove the constraints upon their desired consumption path. Likewise, individuals enter into many contractual savings schemes, such as house purchase on mortgage, life insurance and so forth which cannot be radically altered or abandoned overnight. Similar considerations suggest that consumption and not solely savings will respond to temporary fluctuations in disposable income.

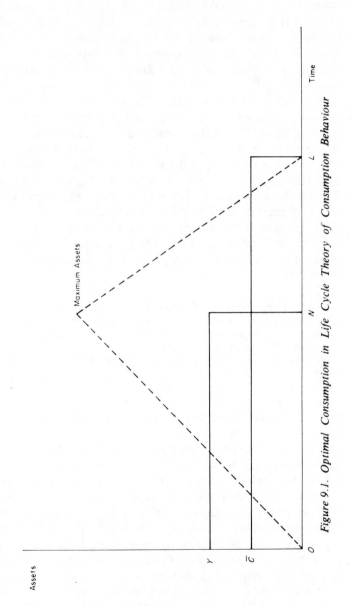

Figure 9.1. *Optimal Consumption in Life Cycle Theory of Consumption Behaviour*

So far, we have avoided the question of how expectations are formed with regard to the crucial variable—permanent or life cycle income streams. As we shall see, this issue is fundamental to the macro-economic impact of tax changes and the substitution of rational, as opposed to adaptive expectations formation, carries important implications for consumption behaviour.

Permanent income or life cycle models of consumer behaviour normally invoke adaptive expectations. Thus, essentially unobservable permanent income streams are derived from past levels of *actual* income, with the more distant income levels exerting a correspondingly weaker effect. It follows that, over time, as actual income changes, the expected permanent income will also change. However, a change in current income will not exert the same effect as suggested by the simpler Keynesian models; its impact upon consumption will be 'diluted' on account of its being but one part of a whole series of income streams determining current expenditure outlays. In Friedman's (1957) terms:

'current consumption is largely determined by past incomes... the effect is almost certain to be a much smaller estimate of the marginal propensity to consume out of current income... it means that a much larger part of current consumption is interpreted as autonomous.... The result is a smaller investment multiplier and an inherently cyclically more stable system (p. 238).

How is this conclusion changed by the assumption that expectations of permanent income are formed rationally? The answer is quite startling and contradicts the gradual moving average postulate of the adaptive model. This is because, when expectations are formed rationally, individuals should not expect that their estimate of permanent income will alter due to a revised weighting given to past experience. All past influences, together with any current information, will already have been incorporated into the rational expectation of permanent income. The only reason why the estimate of permanent income should change is on account of some sudden unanticipated change in the current period. Now such changes can be and often are very substantial. Far from being swamped under the influence of past period experiences, they may lead to a complete revision of expected permanent income, especially when the unanticipated shock is itself expected to be permanent.

To illustrate, the OPEC oil price shocks of 1973 and 1979 implied, for net oil importing economies, a permanent reduction in real incomes, at least for foreseeable future periods. Such impacts would generate a major downward revision of the expectation of permanent income (assuming, of course, that such shocks were entirely unanticipated), which would exert immediate repercussions upon planned consumption outlays. In this case, a completely new piece of information generates a fundamental reappraisal of the rational expectation of permanent income. In contrast, under the assumption of adaptive expectations, whilst such an occurrence would reduce permanent income, its initial effect would be muted since the currently observed 'shock' price is but one piece of a lagged data series conditioning current expectations. Thus, whereas the permanent income/life cycle hypothesis had initially suggested that Keynesian claims of volatility and large responses were overstated, this conclusion is now negated once adaptive expectations are replaced by rational expectations. It is not, therefore, the permanent/life cycle hypothesis itself which is of crucial importance here (and to which the majority of economists would subscribe in one form or another) but rather the expectations formation underlying the determination of permanent/life cycle income.

Finally, it may be noted that the sensitivity of consumption to the changed prospect of future income streams will be greater the lower the rate of interest. This is because permanent income is, of course, the *discounted* value of future expected income streams. Accordingly, a revised view of one's future income prospects will imply a greater impact upon the estimation of permanent income, and hence upon planned consumption outlays, the lower the rate of interest and *vice versa*.

How does the inclusion of rational expectations in the derivation of permanent income affect the role to be ascribed to tax policy? First of all, it will be appreciated that we are here concerned only with *unexpected* or *unanticipated* changes in taxation. Any tax change which had been expected would already have been discounted and incorporated into the rational expectation of permanent income. Moreover, transitory tax changes which are expected to be reversed later will generate no change in permanent income and hence will exert no impact upon consumption outlays. Our concern then is essentially with an unanticipated tax change which is believed to be permanent. A permanent unexpected tax reduction, for example, will generate an increase in permanent income and stimulate consumption spending, thus raising the level of aggregate demand. The consequences for real output and employment will then depend upon the assumptions made with respect to the elasticity of the aggregate supply schedule as we indicated in Chapter 4. Let us assume that, owing to the existence of predetermined wage contracts which cannot immediately be renegotiated in response to any price change, in the short run the aggregate supply schedule is relatively price elastic. Thus, initially, although some of the fiscal stimulus will find expression in increased prices, it will also generate increased output and employment. This is the consequence of the increased consumption spending emanating from revised estimates of permanent income. However, in conventional analysis contervailing influences are also brought into play. With a given money stock, the combined increase in both prices and output will imply higher rates of interest, thus 'crowding out' a certain portion of investment outlays. The increase in aggregate demand is thus less than the induced increase in consumption spending, and this is one reason why many commentators have remained sceptical of the potency of fiscal expansion.

However, rational expectations theory also points to reasons why such 'crowding out' may be mitigated or even completely offset. If unanticipated fiscal expansion generates inflationary expectations, economic agents will be induced to economise upon their holdings of money balances, thus bringing about a situation akin to an increase in the money supply. In a formal model along these lines, Hall (1978a) concludes that tax reduction can have a stronger expansionary effect than in similar models based on naive or adaptive expectations. If the demand for money is highly interest-elastic, real output in the short run may increase by more than the induced increase in consumption spending owing to the favourable repercussion upon investment outlays. In short, 'the introduction of rational expectations to a macroeconomic model does not always make it more classical or monetarist in its behaviour.'

NOTES

1   The argument here refers to the changed composition of portfolio holdings of the private sector which generates a demand for money to restore equilibrium. See, for example, Peacock and Shaw (1981).
2   It is, of course, necessary to distinguish between consumption and expenditures upon consumption goods when the later include durable consumer goods.
3   For an analysis of competing theories of consumer behaviour see Greenaway and Shaw (1983).
4   The classic reference here is to the temporary 1968 income tax surcharge imposed in the United States during the Vietnam War. See Springer (1975, 1977) and Okun (1977).

APPENDIX: MONETARY NEUTRALITY AND TAX NON-NEUTRALITY

As is well known, taxes can influence allocation decisions by altering relative rates of return. It is, therefore, of interest to note that a monetary change which is fully translated into price level changes, and which is therefore normally considered neutral, may, because of associated tax repercussions, generate non-neutral effects. This point has been made forcibly by Feldstein (1976, 1980) and can perhaps be best illustrated by invoking one of his examples.

In a zero inflation condition, let both nominal and real rates of interest be 4 per cent. If interest income is taxable at a rate of 50 per cent, the real net of tax return to saving is accordingly 2 per cent. Now suppose the zero inflation rate is transformed into a 6 per cent inflation rate. Following upon our illustration of Chapter 1, nominal interest rates will rise to 10 per cent to leave real rates unchanged. This is one interpretation of the neutrality of monetary policy; each 1 per cent rise in the rate of

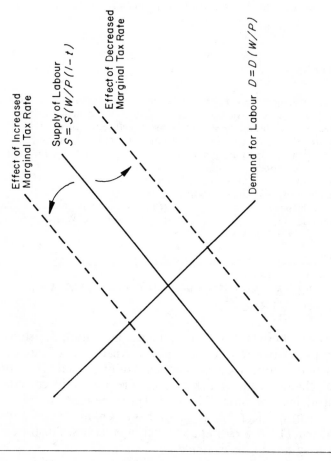

Figure 9.2. Labour Supply Shifts Following Inflation Induced Changes in Marginal Tax Rates

expected inflation will generate a 1 per cent rise in nominal rates of interest. Clearly, however, with tax rates unchanged, the real net of tax return on saving has been reduced to *minus* 1 per cent. The identical argument applies to the reduction in the real cost of borrowing if we assume that one is able to offset nominal interest payments against tax liability. Surely, such changes in real net of tax returns and real net of tax borrowing costs will generate *real* effects upon decisions to save and invest.

Similar arguments pertain to progressive income tax structures unless tax brackets are index linked. An anticipated change in the money supply which is immediately translated into uniform price inflation throughout the entire economy, including factor markets, will push employees into higher marginal tax brackets — in effect decreasing real net of tax take-home pay. If the demand for labour is a function of the pre-tax real wage, whilst labour supply is a function of the post-tax real wage, then every such inflation induced change in the marginal rate of tax will shift the labour supply curve as indicated in Figure 9.2. An apparently neutral monetary policy is associated with real impacts upon employment and output levels in the economy.

10 Rational Expectations: Assessment and Critique

A substantial portion of the rational expectations theory is readily conceded at the outset. The basic idea, namely that economic agents do not merely extrapolate from the historical record, must, on purely empirical grounds, be judged correct. That individual agents do, in some measure or another, take the policy statements of the authorities into account in forming their expectations is equally uncontroversial. That economic agents may learn from past experience is also unlikely to meet fundamental dissent—although a sceptic might justifiably question the rapidity of the learning process. Moreover, no one would seriously dispute that the private sector, in the aggregate, will alter its mode of behaviour in the light of government interventionist policy.

It must also be admitted that the rational expectations thesis is superior to any competing statement of expectations formation since it is explicitly stated in terms of utility maximising behaviour. Alternative theories of expectations formation, such as adaptive expectations, have the virtue of simplicity and are easy to incorporate into economic models and simulation exercises but they fail the one acid test—they do not conform with the basic principles of maximising behaviour.

In contrast, rational expectations doctrine conforms closely with the predilections of *homo economicus*. It assumes that individuals are rational, possess an interest in acquiring information and use that information efficiently in order to avoid making costly mistakes. If mistakes are made they will not be systematic. Further, it assumes that agents do not knowingly leave profitable opportunities unexploited. In brief, it claims that economic agents are self-interested and act accordingly, and it would be strange indeed if such an assumption did not find sympathy in the mind of the average economist.

It must also be conceded that the doctrine of rational expectations has received considerable empirical support from the study of specialised financial markets and commodity exchanges. Such markets, usually characterised as efficient markets, incorporate all available information, past experience and current information into the prevailing price. What this means is that economic theory *per se* is of no value to speculators engaged in the attempt to predict future price movements since that theory is already a determinant of the current price. What would be of value would be additional information; it is for this reason that in such markets agents go to great lengths to obtain adequate and reliable information. As we have seen, this is the essence of the rational expectations hypothesis.

Nonetheless, objections to the rational expectations hypothesis continue to be raised. Essentially, these can be divided into two distinct categories. Upon the one hand, there are those economists who question whether within the context of a highly complex, interdependent and changing economy individuals do in fact form expectations rationally and whether the economy can and does conform to the rational expectations equilibrium path as implied by the theory. Upon the other hand, there are those economists, often quite sympathetic to the underlying philosophy, who dispute the implications derived from rational expectations doctrine when combined with alternative assumptions such as the assumption of almost unlimited price flexibility.

With regard to the first class of objection, the following points are invariably raised. Economic agents may not possess the means to acquire and process information in the manner required by the theory. Even if we meet this objection by delegating information collecting and processing to 'specialist' bodies and institutions possessed of a comparative advantage in this area, it does not necessarily imply that human behaviour will respond in accordance with it. Shiller (1978) makes this point explicitly in the following way:

Can these authors seriously believe that unemployed workers really know this data or use professional forecasts which make use of this data optimally? If anyone believes this, he should take a trip to the nearest unemployment compensation office and ask people standing in line for the latest data on the growth of the money supply, the government surplus, or the latest inflation forecast of an econometric model. (p. 36).

Of course, this type of objection does not deny the weaker version of the rational expectations thesis. It merely indicates that many individuals find it not worth their while to acquire pertinent information, and for many participants in the market economy this may well be perfectly sensible behaviour. However, it does suggest that the expectations formation mechanism is a long way removed from the 'mathematical expectation conditional upon all information'. This leads naturally into a second line of criticism which suggests that not all markets will behave in the same way. Whilst stock markets and similar markets may be efficient and act in accordance with rational expectations theory because the incentive to do so is there, other markets, especially labour markets, may find an alternative form of behaviour more favourable. This point has been made most forcibly by Arrow (1978):

Economic theory implies that price anticipations are relevant in decisions about capital formation but not in flow decisions. In allocating consumption today, the future price of a completely perishable good is irrelevant. . . . An extreme example of a perishable commodity is labour time. The labourer is durable, but the hours he can work are not. Hence, there is essentially no reason for anticipations of future wage increases, correct or incorrect, to affect the present supply of labour. Yet one finds models which argue that statistical unemployment is wholly or partly a voluntary withholding of labour because of unduly optimistic expectations (p. 18).

It may well be the case that given all the complexities of a highly modernised interdependent economy, some expectations will be formed rationally and others will be formed in a much less elaborate manner. 'Rational' reasons may dictate non-rational expectations formation. Rational expectations formation would be most appropriate in conditions where large amounts of information are readily available at minimal cost and where considerable costs attach to not invoking such information. Foreign exchange markets, stock markets and other financial markets obviously meet this criterion but labour markets may not. Especially when contractual obligations delay adjustment processes and where false trading does not disadvantage the already employed worker the rational expectations adjustment may be found wanting.[1] Where divergent expectations exist, being rational in some markets, adaptive in others and still more naive in others, many of the standard conclusions of the rational expectations thesis are rendered untenable.

A further source of concern turns upon the ability of the macro-economy to conform to the equilibrium rational expectations path. The difficulty here is the ability of economic agents to learn to adapt to a new policy measure imposed by government. Initially, forecasts of the future may be extremely unreliable in the light of a new unknown policy measure and time will be needed to learn the true impact of the measure upon the economy. This will itself be no simple matter since the unreliable expectations formed in the light of the new measure will, in turn, affect the progress of the economy. Nonetheless, it is a cardinal assumption of rational expectations theory that economic agents cannot be fooled all the time and that ultimately the economy must conform, in the light of a continuous learning process, to the rational expectations equilibrium, by which time the effect of the policy measure is entirely negated. If all agents do indeed form their expectations rationally, then this conclusion must follow as a matter of logic. However, this learning process may take a considerable amount of time and before it is complete the policy regime and the policy measure may have changed yet again. Such changes are quite additional to structural or institutional changes which occur naturally as the economy evolves and which also impart a need to re-learn the adjustment processess. It is plausible that the rational expectations equilibrium is never attained. Shiller (1978) has outlined the problem in graphic terms:

Suppose there has been a sudden major change in policy, for example, suppose Phase I controls have just been instituted. Now forecasters must start from scratch in formulating forecasting equations. ... One must wait perhaps 15 or 20 quarters in order to have enough observations for a regression of any value. After 20 quarters, the revised expectations mechanism may now be used, and doing so will again change the structure of the economy so the expectations mechanism must be estimated again. It may then take another 15 or 20 quarters before regressions reveal the change in the optimal forecasting mechanism. ... It may take a very long time before the economy will converge on a rational expectations equilibrium and before this happens there may be another major change in the economy (p. 39).

Let us now turn to the second class of arguments which concern themselves more with the policy implications derived from rational expectations theory than with the underlying concept itself. That is to say, the objections are more clearly directed against the new classical macro-economics as opposed to the doctrine of rational expectations *per se*.

The first, and in many respects the most fundamental point, concerns the distinction between *predictable systematic* policy measures of government and *unpredictable unsystematic* changes in monetary and fiscal policy. The former do not, it is argued, affect real variables whilst the latter do; indeed it is upon this latter assertion that rational expectation theorists have provided an explanation of the business cycle which incorporates the commonly observed characteristics of pro-cyclical movements in prices and output.[2]

The question which must be raised, however, is whether, as a matter of practicality, it is possible to make a rigid distinction between systematic and unsystematic policy action. Does the government itself possess the power to make systematic or consistent policy actions which are not themselves tainted by association with unintended and thus unsystematic accompanying changes in monetary and fiscal variables? The experience of the British economy in recent years vividly highlights this point. The Conservative government returned in 1979 had decidedly monetarist leanings. It believed, quite sincerely, that control of inflation was the number one priority objective. It argued, with an engaging simplicity, that the objective could best be secured be control of the money supply. It concluded, rather more mysteriously, that this control could be attained by controlling the size of the PSBR.[3] Thus, tax and expenditure plans were to be set so as to generate the PSBR outturn figure consistent with the attainment of the money supply target. In short, the reign of Keynesianism was over; fiscal policy had become fully subordinated to the pursuit of monetary targets.

In practice, of course, unexpectedly large increases in unemployment depleted fiscal revenues and raised expenditure outlays so that the PSBR figures displayed a substantial degree of endogeneity. Now if government monetary changes encompass both an exogenous (controllable) and endogenous (non-controllable) component, one might logically question the ability of private economic agents to perceive which is which. Certainly, it is reasonable to assume that different economic agents will possess different perceptions as to what was a systematic and predictable policy change. When systematic and unsystematic monetary changes interact, economic agents might differ in their interpretation—especially when *ex post* political expediency dictates the claim that policies were totally systematic and consistent all along! If economic agents do differ in this way, then they will differ as to the likely consequences of the policies themselves and, therefore, will differ in their response pattern to those policies.

This leads naturally to a second critique of the rational expectations thesis, namely that all economic agents possess the same fundamental model of how the economy actually operates. Quite apart from the fact that the model in question is invariably a *simpliste* quantity theory model, it is patently obvious that numerous models co-exist side by side, each offering a distinct forecast of the future progress of the economy. In the UK, for example, there are no less than five major forecasting models regularly quoted and highly influential in conditioning public expectations.[4] Of course, one could argue that if the end purpose of economic enquiry and investigation is to seek an understanding of how the economy actually behaves, then ultimately one explanation should prevail. Theories unsupported or denied by the empirical findings will be discarded so that competing theories will be whittled down until only one dominant theory—the correct theory—remains. The rational expectations theorist may take this approach and argue that *ultimately* all economic agents will be possessed of the identical and correct model. Maybe so—although the argument is by no means immediately obvious. Even the most sophisticated econometric techniques may not be able to distinguish conclusively between rival theoretical propositions regardless of the excellence of the data. There are also methodological problems concerning the refutation or denial of 'false' hypotheses.[5] Even if we were to accept the inevitability of the one universal theory, however, the fact remains that at present we are a long way from such a consensus. Until that time arrives, different economic agents will possess different ideas of eventual outcomes, and thus their collective ability to negate *systematic* government policies is accordingly blunted. Indeed, once this diversity is recognised, economic agents in the aggregate may, intentionally or otherwise, reinforce the intention of the policy measure.

A related argument concerning the private sector's response to countercyclical policy may be entered here. Perception that the government is pursuing a sensible and consistent countercyclical policy may promote confidence within the private sector and generate the belief that fluctuations in prices and output from their accepted 'norm' will be contained within reasonably tolerable limits. The private sector is most assuredly taking account of government macro-economic policy, as rational expectations theory claims, but in the present case what is being asserted is that the confidence gained generates more stable private sector behaviour, which in itself promotes the attainment of stabilisation goals.

Perhaps the strongest challenge to the new classical macro-economics is that it appears to generate conclusions in conflict with observed reality. As R.A. Gordon (1976) suggests, rational expectations is an illustration of the way in which 'theory proceeds with impeccable logic from unrealistic assumptions to conclusions that contradict the historical record.' One of the difficulties here concerns the persistence of the business cycle. In a world of rational expectations, all expectational errors would be randomly distributed over time and, if this is the case, then output and unemployment would be uncorrelated over time. But this is indeed not the case. A high degree of serial correlation obtains. Typically, recessions last a long time and years of unemployment (below the natural level) are then superseded by years of over-full employment (above the natural level). Attempts to explain such patterns of cyclical persistence in terms of informational lags (Lucas, 1975) are not very persuasive, especially when rational expectations theory itself relies in large measure upon the existence of virtually free information stemming from government and media agencies. Attempts to explain the persistence problem have usually relied upon the costs of adjustment. Low output and employment levels in one year generate similar levels in the subsequent year, it is argued, because of the costs associated with the return to 'normal' output levels. Clearly, there is some force in this argument if it is applied to relatively short periods, but it is far less convincing as an explanation of recessionary periods lasting three or four years or so.

The policy ineffectiveness proposition of new classical macro-economics is also called into question by the historical record. It is surely the case that stabilisation policies have been more successful in the post-1945 Keynesian period, in terms of mitigating fluctuations, than in any other period during the present century. This is undeniably true for the United States and one might make a similar claim for the United Kingdom, although in the latter case output and employment have often been sacrificed to balance of payments objectives.

Perhaps the most damaging aspect of the real world economy for the relevance of the conclusions emanating from rational expectations theory turns upon the existence of price and wage inflexibility. We have already indicated reasons why rational economic agents *might* opt in favour of fixed price agreements over relatively long periods. Quite apart from such maximising strategy, however, the very existence of rigidities from *whatever* source makes it perfectly possible for consistent macro-economic policy, even when fully anticipated, still to be non-neutral in its impact upon real variables.

An example of rigidity is found in the 1973 OPEC price rise. For net oil importing economies such a substantial increase in the price of oil (an autonomous 'shock') implied an immediate once-and-for-all decline in real income—reflected by an inward shift of the aggregate supply curve. If full employment were to be maintained, real wages would have to fall. Also, relative prices would have to change, with oil intensive products experiencing a relative increase in price and non-oil intensive products a relative decline. From the vantage point of rational expectations theory, what is required is for all economic agents, including monopoly entrenched trade unions, voluntarily and virtually instantaneously to enter into price adjustment activity so as to bring about a new equilibrium with the minimum of delay. However, this is not the way in which real world economic agents chose to operate. Trade unions resisted money wage cuts. Suppliers of non-oil intensive produce resisted the comparative price decline required which would have imperilled their real living standards. Initially, then the attempt was made to hold prices firm and the whole weight of adjustment was thrown upon the side of quantity changes—a situation of false trading. The consequence, of course, would be for a substantial amount of unemployment to be generated, especially in the non-oil intensive sector. Indeed, it was in recognition of the fact that the consequences for unemployment would be severe that governments chose to intervene. By raising the level of monetary demand, they were able to maintain employment levels at the prevailing money wage rate whilst allowing the resultant price inflation to bring about the required reduction in real incomes.

It seems unrealistic to assume, as rational expectations theorists are wont to do, that all prices are market clearing prices, implying that all unemployment is essentially voluntary. An alternative way of saying this is that it appears unrealistic to assume away the existence of money illusion, as rational expectations theory would suggest. The evidence would more readily suggest that money illusion is a fact of life. Economic agents do not always perceive how their *real* economic situation has been transformed by changed circumstances, especially when the new circumstance is unique. Until this perception fully dawns, they suffer a money illusion which generates a false understanding of the true economic value of the services they have to offer. It is, of course, true that money illusion will ultimately be eliminated by the harsh light of painful experience, but its elimination can take time. Moreover, the elimination of money illusion upon one occasion in response to a changed circumstance does not rule out its existence in relation to a totally different experience. For example, in the inflation which characterised the late 1960s and 1970s it appeared that nominal interest rates paralleled inflation rates more closely than had been the case in previous periods, suggesting that economic agents were overcoming money illusion more efficiently. But this does not rule out money illusion on the same scale in the future, or even negative real interest rates following a period of relative price stability.

Finally, the rational expectations hypothesis exhibits a remarkably optimistic view of human nature. Individuals are endowed with remarkable learning ability and infallible memories. Accurate perceptions do not fade with the passage of time. It seems crucial to the policy implications of the rational expectations doctrine that experiences learned from one inflationary episode remain vividly intact even after long periods of price stability. Like the proverbial elephant, our economic agent never forgets. Moreover, this knowledge gained in the light of experience appears to be transmitted inter-generationally at zero cost. In practice, of course, the rational expectations philosophy would suggest that different agents have different expectations according to the length of time they have been participating in labour and product markets. What is more (and this is in many ways the most questionable assertion of all), it is assumed that the knowledge and experience acquired can be applied correctly so as to obtain the 'correct' expectation even in the case of essentially *unique* events. Would that it were so!

In summary, rational expectations theory has improved our understanding of expectations formation and has seriously questioned the usefulness of modelling alternative expectational theories in econometric models. It has led to an increased scepticism concerning the efficacy of Keynesian oriented 'trade-off' policies by providing convincing reasons why such policies will become less and less effective the longer inflation lasts and the more money illusion is eroded. In part, it reinforces the case for reliance upon automatic stabilisers, fiscal or monetary. It has yet to demonstrate, however, that there is no case for *predictable* macro-economic interventionist policies.

NOTES

1   Efficient markets, such as the stock market, conform rapidly to the market clearing price since all market participants have the incentive, by buying and selling, to exploit profitable opportunities presented by non-market clearing price situations. However, this need not apply to the market for labour. The employed worker, seeing that the current wage is in excess of that which would clear the market, has no incentive to negotiate a wage reduction.

2   See especially Lucas (1975).

3   The Public Sector Borrowing Requirement. For present purposes, we may identify this with the size of the budget deficit. For more precise definition and for arguments relating it to the control of the money supply see Peacock and Shaw (1981).

4   These are: The Treasury Model, the National Institute Model, The London Business School Model, The Liverpool Model and the Cambridge Economic Policy Group Model, and encompass a wide variety of differing economic philosophies.

5   The argument here refers to the Duhem-Quine thesis which argues that it is not possible to refute single hypotheses since the introduction of additional hypotheses might be able to salvage the original hypothesis from refutation. Thus, for example, it we have a theory suggesting that monetary growth will generate inflation, whilst our observation reveals that monetary growth was followed by price stability, a secondary thesis linking output growth to monetary growth could salvage the original hypothesis. For an introductory statement of the Duhem-Quine thesis see Cross (1982a) and at a more advanced level Cross (1982b).

Suggestions for Further Reading

The literature on rational expectations is now extremely extensive. Unfortunately, the vast bulk of it is pitched at such a technical level and assumes such a prior knowledge of theoretical macro-economics as to be outside the general competence of the reader to whom this book is addressed. The following recommendations, in contrast, focus upon contributions which are relatively non-technical and presume little more than a solid grounding in national income determination and which do not require a knowledge of econometric techniques.

Introductory-intermediate level textbooks dealing with rational expectations include Parkin and Bade (1982) and Greenaway and Shaw (1983). Relatively simple and perceptive introductory surveys of the thesis are presented by Haberler (1980) and Mayes (1981). Elementary introductory statements dealing with various aspects of the rational expectations controversy by distinguished contributors including McCallum, Baily, Lucas and Sargent are to be found in the admirable little volume edited by Baily and Okun (1982). Maddock and Carter (1982) offer a 'Child's Guide' which complements much of the discussion here; however, the child in question is comparatively well versed in neo-Keynesian and monetarist controversies. A useful survey of the evolution of thought on rational expectations is provided by Kantor (1979), whilst Grossman (1980), in an introductory chapter to the volume by Fischer (1980), surveys the business cycle and policy implications of the doctrine. One of the most authoritative reviews of the earlier expectations literature is given in R.J.

Gordon (1976). The entire November issue of the *Journal of Money Credit and Banking*, Part 2 (1980) is devoted to a series of papers on rational expectations. Many of these are of a technical nature but some of the comments from the very distinguished participants are not. Noteworthy in this regard are the contributions of Tobin, Cagan and Okun, amongst others.

Finally, the volume by Begg (1982b) is quite excellent and is a useful source of reference; it is not, however, what it claims to be in that it requires more, and a good deal more, than 'a knowledge only of introductory macroeconomics and elementary mathematics'. Less demanding is the volume by Scheffrin (1983).

Bibliography

Abel, Andrew B. and Mishkin, Frederic S. (1983) 'An Integrated View of Tests of Rationality, Market Efficiency and the Short-Run Neutrality of Monetary Policy', *Journal of Monetary Economics*, January.

Alchian, Armen A. (1969) 'Information Costs, Pricing and Resource Unemployment', *Western Economic Journal*, June.

Ando, Albert, and Modigliani, Franco (1963) 'The "Life Cycle" Hypothesis of Saving: Aggregate Implications and Tests', *American Economic Review*, March.

Arrow, Kenneth J. (1978) 'The Future and the Present in Economic Life', *Economic Inquiry*, April.

Artis, M. (1979) 'Recent Developments in the Theory of Fiscal Policy: A Survey', in Cook and Jackson (eds), *Current Issues in Fiscal Policy*, Martin Robertson.

Baily, Martin N. and Okun, Arthur M. (eds) (1982) *The Battle Against Unemployment and Inflation*, New York, W.W. Norton & Company.

Barro, R.J. (1974) 'Are Government Bonds Net Wealth', *Journal of Political Economy*, November-December.

Barro, R.J. (1976) 'Rational Expectations and the Role of Monetary Policy', *Journal of Monetary Economics*, January.

Barro, R.J. (1977a) 'Long Term Contracting, Sticky Prices and Monetary Policy', *Journal of Monetary Economics*, July.

Barro, R.J. (1977b) 'Unanticipated Money Growth and Unemployment in the United States', *American Economic Review*, March.

Barro, R.J. (1978) 'Unanticipated Money, Output and the Price Level in the United States', *Journal of Political Economy*, August.

Barro, R.J. (1979) 'Second Thoughts on Keynesian Economics', *American Economic Review*, May.

Barro, R.J. (1980) 'Federal Deficit Policy and the Effects of Public Debt Stocks', *Journal of Money Credit and Banking*, Part 2, November.

Barro, R.J. (1981) *Money, Expectations and Business Cycles: Essays in Macroeconomics*, New York, Academic Press.

Barro, R.J. and Fischer S. (1976) 'Recent Developments in Monetary Theory', *Journal of Monetary Economics*, April.

Barro, R.J. and Grossman H.I. (1976) *Money, Employment and Inflation*, Cambridge, Cambridge University Press.

Barro, R.J. and Rush, Mark (1980) 'Unanticipated Money and Economic Activity', in Fisher (ed.).

Beenstock, M. (1980) *A Neo-Classical Analysis of Macro-Economic Policy*, Cambridge, Cambridge University Press, esp. Ch. 8.

Begg, D.K.H. (1980) 'Rational Expectations and the Non-Neutrality of Systematic Monetary Policy', *Review of Economic Studies*.

Begg, D.K.H. (1982a) 'Rational Expectations, Wage Rigidity and Involuntary Unemployment', *Oxford Economic Papers*.

Begg, D.K.H. (1982b) *The Rational Expectations Revolution in Macroeconomics Theories and Evidence*, Oxford, Philip Allan.

Bilson, J.F.O. (1980) 'The Rational Expectations Approach to the Consumption Function: A Multi-Country Study', *European Economic Review*, Vol. 13.

Black, Stanley (1972) 'The Use of Rational Expectations in Models of Speculation', *Review of Economics and Statistics*, May.

Bliss, Christopher (1983) 'Two views of Macroeconomics', *Oxford Economic Papers*, March.

Boltho, Andrea (1983) 'Is Western Europe Caught in an "Expectations Trap"?', *Lloyds Bank Review*, April.

Brainard, W.C. and Cooper, R.N. (1975) 'Empirical Monetary Macroeconomics: What Have We Learned in the Last 25 years?', *American Economic Review*, May.

Brunner, Karl (1970) 'The Monetarist Revolution in Monetary Theory', *Weltwirtschaftliches Archiv*, 105, No. 1.

Brunner, K., Cukierman, A. and Meltzer, A.H. (1980) 'Stagflation, Persistent Unemployment and the Permanence of Economic Shocks', *Journal of Monetary Economics*, October.

Buiter, W.H. (1980) 'The Macroeconomics of Dr. Pangloss: A Critical Survey of the New Classical Macroeconomics', *Economic Journal*, March.

Buiter, W.H. (1981) 'The Superiority of Contingent Rules over Fixed Rules in Models with Rational Expectations, *Economic Journal*, September.

Buiter, W.H. and Miller, Marcus (1981) 'The Thatcher Experiment: The First Two Years', *Brookings Papers on Economic Activity*, No. 2.

Burmeister, Edwin (1980) 'Some Conceptual Issues in Rational Expectations Modelling', *Journal of Money Credit and Banking*, Part 2, November.

Bray, Margaret (1981) 'Futures Trading, Rational Expectations and the Efficient markets hypothesis', *Econometrica*.

Cagan, Phillip (1956) 'The Monetary Dynamics of Hyperinflation', in *Studies in the Quantity Theory of Money* Milton Friedman (ed.) Chicago, University of Chicago Press.

Cagan, Phillip (1979) *Persistent Inflation*. New York, Columbia University Press.

Cagan, Phillip (1980) "Reflections on Rational Expectations", *Journal of Money Credit and Banking, Part 2,* November.

Carlson, G.A. and Parkin, J.M. (1975) 'Inflation Expectations', *Economica*, May.

Clements, K.W. and Jonson, P.D. (1979) 'Unanticipated Money, Disequilibrium Modelling and Rational Expectations', *Economic Letters*, No. 2.

Cross, R.B. (1982a) *Economic Theory and Policy in the U.K.*, Oxford, Martin Robertson.

Cross, R.B. (1982b) 'The Duhem–Levine Thesis, Lakatos and the Appraisal of Theories in Macroeconomics', *Economic Journal*, June.

Cuthbertson K. (1980) 'The Determination of Expenditure on Consumer Durables', *National Institute Economic Review*,

Cyert, Richard M. and DeGrout M.H. (1974) 'Rational Expectations and Bayesian Analysis', *Journal of Political Economy*, May/June.

Daly, George G. and Mayor, Thomas H. (1983) 'Reason and Rationality during Energy Crises', *Journal of Political Economy*, February.

Darby, M.R. (1976) 'Three-and-a-half Million U.S. Employees Have Been Mislaid, or an Explanation of Unemployment, 1934–41', *Journal of Political Economy*, February.

DeCanio, S. (1979) 'Rational Expectations and Learning from Experience', *Quarterly Journal of Economics*.

Dornbusch, R. (1976) 'Expectations and Exchange Rate Dynamics', *Journal of Political Economy*, December.

Drazen, Allan (1980) 'Recent Developments in Macroeconomic Disequilibrium Theory', *Econometrica*, March.

Fair, R.C. (1978) 'A Criticism of One Class of Macro-Economic Models with Rational Expectations', *Journal of Money Credit and Banking*.

Fair, R.C. (1979a) 'On Modelling the Effects of Government Policies', *American Economic Review*, May.

Fair, R.C. (1979b) 'An Analysis of the Accuracy of Four Macroeconomic Models', *Journal of Political Economy*, August.

Fama, Eugene F. (1970) 'Efficient Capital Markets: A Review of Theory and Empirical Work', *Journal of Finance*, May.

Federal Reserve Bank of Atlanta (1982) *Supply-Side Economics in the 1980's*, Conference Proceedings, Westport, Conn., Quorum Books.

Feigie, Edgar L., and Pearce Douglas K. (1976) 'Economically Rational Expectations: Are Innovations in the Rate of Inflation Independent of Innovations in Measures of Monetary and Fiscal Policy?', *Journal of Political Economy*, June.

Feldstein, Martin (1976) 'Inflation, Income Taxes and the Rate of Interest: A Theoretical analysis', *American Economic Review*.

Feldstein, Martin (1980) 'Comment' in Fischer (ed.).

Fellner, William (1976) *Towards a Reconstruction of Macroeconomics*, Washington, D.C., American Enterprise Institute for Public Policy Research.

Fellner, William (1979) 'The Credibility Effect and Rational Expectations: Implications of the Gramlich Study', *Brookings Papers on Economic Activity*, 1.

Fellner, William (1980) 'The Valid Case of Rationality Hypotheses in the Theory of Expectations', *Journal of Money Credit and Banking*, Part 2.

Fellner, William (1982) 'Economic Theory amidst Political Currents: The Spreading Interest in Monetarism and in the Theory of Market Expectations', *Welt Wirtschaftliches Archiv*, No. 3.

Fischer, Stanley, (1977) 'Long-Term Constraints, Rational Expectations, and the Optimal Money Supply Rate', *Journal of Political Economy*, February.

Fischer, Stanley (ed.) (1980) *Rational Expectations and Economic Policy*, National Bureau of Economic Research, Chicago, University of Chicago Press.

Frenkel, J. (1975) 'Inflation and the Formation of Expectations', *Journal of Monetary Economics*, October.

Friedman, Benjamin M. (1979) 'Optimal Expectations and the Extreme Information Assumptions of "Rational Expectations" Macro-Models', *Journal of Monetary Economics*, January.

Friedman, Milton (1957) *A Theory of the Consumption Function*, Princeton, Princeton University Press.

Friedman, Milton (1968) 'The Role of Monetary Policy', *American Economic Review*, March.

Friedman, Milton and Heller, Walter M. (1969) *Monetary versus fiscal Policy: A Dialogue*, New York, Norton and Co.

Friedman, Milton (1977) *Inflation and Unemployment: The New Dimension of Politics*, London, Institute of Economic Affairs, Occasional Paper 51.

Frish, H. (1977) 'Inflation Theory 1963–75: A Second Generation Survey', *Journal of Economic Literature*, December.

Gomes, Gustavo Maia (1982) 'Irrationality of "Rational Expectations"', *Journal of Post-Keynesian Economics*, Fall.

Gordon, Robert Aaron (1976) 'Rigour and Relevance in a Changing Institutional Setting', *American Economic Review*, March.

Gordon, Robert J. (1976) 'Recent Developments in the Theory of Inflation and Unemployment', *Journal of Monetary Economics*, April.

Gordon, Robert J. (1980) 'Postwar Macroeconomics: The Evolution of Events and Ideas', in Feldstein, Martin (ed.) *The American Economy*, Chicago, University of Chicago Press.

Gordon, Robert J. (1981) 'Output Fluctuations and Gradual Price Adjustment', *Journal of Economic Literature*, June.

Gramlich, E.M. (1979) 'Macroeconomic Policy Response to Price Shocks', *Brooking Papers on Economic Activity*, No. 1.

Greenaway, David and Shaw, G.K. (1983) *Macro-Economics: Theory and Policy in the U.K.*, Oxford, Martin Robertson.

Grossman, H.I. (1979) 'Why does Aggregate Employment Fluctuate?', *American Economic Review*, May.

Grossman, H.I. (1980) 'Rational Expectations, Business Cycles and Government Behaviour', in Fischer (ed.).

Grossman, S.J. and Stiglitz, J.F. (1980) 'On the Impossibility of Informationally Efficient Markets', *American Economic Review*, June.

Haberler, Gottfried (1980) *Notes on Rational and Irrational Expectations*, Reprint No. 111, American Enterprise Institute, March.

Haberler, Gottfried (1982) 'Critical Notes on Rational Expectations', *Journal of Money Credit and Banking*, Part 2, November.

Hahn, F.H. (1980) 'Monetarism and Economic Theory', *Economica*, February.

Hall, R.E. (1976) 'The Phillips Curve and Macroeconomic Policy, in

Brunner, K. and Meltzer, A. (eds) *The Phillips Curve and Labour Markets*, North-Holland.

Hall, R.E. (1978a) 'The Macroeconomic Impact of Changes in Income Taxes in the Short and Medium Runs', *Journal of Political Economy*, Part 2, April.

Hall, R.E. (1978b) 'Stochastic Implications of the Life Cycle-Permanent Income Hypothesis: Theory and Evidence', *Journal of Political Economy*, December.

Hall, R.E. (1980) 'Employment Fluctuations and Wage Rigidity', *Brookings Papers on Economic Activity*, No. 1, Washington.

Hicks, J.R. (1974) *The Crisis in Keynesian Economics*, Oxford, Basil Blackwell.

Holden, K., Peel, D.A. and Thompson J.L. (1983) *Modelling the U.K. Economy: An Introduction*, Oxford, Martin Robertson.

Howitt, P. (1979) 'Evaluating the Non-Market Clearing Approach', *American Economic Review*, May.

Howitt, P. (1981) 'Activist Monetary Policy under Rational Expectations', *Journal of Political Economy*, April.

Kaldor, N. (1972) 'The Irrelevance of Equilibrium Economics', *Economic Journal*, December.

Kantor, Brian (1979) 'Rational Expectations and Economic Thought', *Journal of Economic Literature*, December.

Keynes, J.M. (1921) *A Treatise on Probability*, London, Macmillan.

Keynes, J.M. (1923) *Tract on Monetary Reform*, London, Macmillan.

Keynes, J.M. (1930) *Treatise on Money*, London, Macmillan.

Keynes, J.M. (1936) *The General Theory of Employment Interest and Money*, London, Macmillan.

Keynes, J.M. (1937) 'The General Theory of Employment', *Quarterly Journal of Economics*, February.

Keynes, J.M. (1939) 'Relative Movements of Real Wages and Output', *Economic Journal*, March.

Kregel, J.A. (1976) 'Economic Methodology in the Face of Uncertainty', *Economic Journal*, March.

Kydland, Finn E. and Prescott, Edward C. (1977) 'Rules Rather than Discretion: The Inconsistency of Optimal Plans', *Journal of Political Economy*, June.

Laidler, D.W. (1971) 'The Phillips Curve, Expectations and Incomes Policy', in Johnson, H.G. and Nobay, A.P. (eds) *The Current Inflation*, London, Macmillan.

Laidler, D.W. (1982) *Monetarist Perspectives*, Philip Allan.

Laidler, D.W. and Parkin, M. (1975) 'Inflation: A Survey', *Economic Journal*, December.

Leijonhufvud, Axel (1968) *On Keynesian Economics and The Economics of Keynes*, London, Oxford University Press.

Long, John B. and Plosser, Charles I. (1983) 'Real Business Cycles', *Journal of Political Economy*, February.

Lucas, R.E. Jr. (1972) 'Expectations and the Neutrality of Money', *Journal of Economic Theory*, April.

Lucas, R.E. Jr. (1973) 'Some International Evidence on Output-Inflation Trade Offs', *American Economic Review*, June.

Lucas, R.E. Jr. (1975) 'An Equilibrium Model of the Business Cycle', *Journal of Political Economy*, December.

Lucas, R.E. Jr. (1976) 'Econometric Policy Evaluation: A Critique', *Journal of Monetary Economics*, No. 2, Supplement.

Lucas, R.E. Jr. (1980) 'Methods and Problems in Business Cycle Theory', *Journal of Money, Credit and Banking*, Part 2, November.

Lucas, R.E. Jr. (1981) *Studies in Business-Cycle Theory*, Oxford, Basil Blackwell.

Lucas, R.E. Jr. and Sargent, Thomas J. (1978) 'After Keynesian Macroeconomics', in *After the Phillips Curve: Persistence of High Inflation and High Unemployment*, Federal Reserve Bank of Boston, Conference Series No. 19, 1978, reprinted in Lucas and Sargent (eds) (1981).

Lucas, R.E. Jr. and Sargent, Thomas J. (eds) (1981) *Rational Expectations and Econometric Practice*, London, George Allen and Unwin.

McCallum, Bennett T. (1977) 'Price level Stickiness and the Feasibility of Monetary Stabilisation Policy with Rational Expectations', *Journal of Political Economy*, June.

McCallum, Bennett T. (1978) 'Price Level Adjustments and the Rational Expectations Approach to Macroeconomic Stabilisation Policy', *Journal of Money Credit and Banking*, November.

McCallum, Bennett T. (1979a) 'On the Observational Inequivalence of Classical and Keynesian Models', *Journal of Political Economy*, April.

McCallum, Bennett T. (1979b) 'Monetarism, Rational Expectations Oligopolistic Pricing and the MPS Econometric Model', *Journal of Political Economy*, February.

McCallum, Bennett T. (1979) 'The Current State of the Policy-Ineffectiveness Debate' *American Economic Review*, May, reprinted in Lucas and Sargent (eds) (1981).

McCallum, Bennett T. (1980) 'Rational Expectations and Macroeconomic Stabilisation Policy', *Journal of Money, Credit and Banking*, Part 2, November.

McCallum, Bennett T. (1982) 'Rational Expectations', in Baily, Martin N. and Okun, Arthur M. (eds) *The Battle against Unemployment and Inflation*, 3rd Edition, New York, Norton.

Maddock, Rodney and Carter, Michael (1982) 'A Child's Guide to Rational Expectations', *Journal of Economic Literature*, March.

Maital, Shlomo (1979) 'Inflation Expectations in the Monetarist Black Box', *American Economic Review*, June.

Mayes, David G. (1981) 'The Controversy over Rational Expectations', *National Institute Economic Review*, May.

Maynard, Geoffrey (1982) "Microeconomic Deficiencies in UK Macroeconomic Policy", *Lloyds Bank Review*, July.

Mayor, Thomas (1978) *The Structure of Monetarism*, New York, W.W. Norton.

Minford, Patrick (1980) 'The Nature and Purpose of UK Macroeconomic Models', *Three Banks Review*, March.

Minford, Patrick (1980) 'A Rational Expectations Model of the UK under Fixed and Floating Exchange Rates', in Brunner, K. and Meltzer, A.H. (eds) *The State of Macro-Economics*, Amsterdam, North Holland.

Minford, Patrick and Peel, David (1981) 'The Role of Monetary Stabilisation Policy under Rational Expectations', *Manchester School*, March.

Minford, Patrick and Peel, David (1981) 'Is the Government's Economic Strategy on Course?', *Lloyds Bank Review*, April.

Minford, Patrick and Peel, David (1982) 'The Microfoundations of the Phillips Curve with Rational Expectations', *Oxford Economic Papers*, November.

Mishkin, Frederic S. (1981) 'Monetary Policy and Long Term Interest Rates: An Efficient Markets Approach', *Journal of Monetary Economics*, January.

Mishkin, Frederic S. (1981) 'Are Market Forecasts Rational?', *American Economic Review*, June.

Mishkin, Frederic S. (1982a) 'Does Anticipated Monetary Policy Matter? An Econometric Investigation', *Journal of Political Economy*, February.

Mishkin, Frederic S. (1982b) 'Monetary Policy and Short-Term Interest Rates: An Efficient Markets Rational Expectations Approach', *Journal of Finance*, March.

Mishkin, Frederic S. (1982c) 'Does Anticipated Aggregate Demand Policy Matter? Further Econometric Results', *American Economic Review*, September.

Mishkin, Frederic S. (1982/83) 'A Rational Expectations Approach to Macroeconometrics', National Bureau of Economic Research *Reporter*, Winter.

Mishkin, Frederic S. (1983) *A Rational Expectations Approach to Macroeconometrics: Testing Policy Ineffectiveness or Efficient Market Models*, Chicago, University of Chicago Press for National Bureau of Economic Research.

Modigliani, Franco and Grunberg, Emils (1954) 'The Predictability of Social Events', *Journal of Political Economy*, December.

Modigliani, Franco (1966) 'The Life Cycle Hypothesis of Saving, the Demand for Wealth and the Supply of Capital', *Social Research*, Vol. 33, No. 2.

Modigliani, Franco (1977) 'The Monetarist Controversy or Should We Foresake Stabilisation Policies', *American Economic Review*, March.

Muth, J. (1961) 'Rational Expectations and the Theory of Price Movements', *Econometrica*, July.

Nerlove, M. (1958) 'Adaptive Expectations and Cobweb Phenomena', *Quarterly Journal of Economics*, May.

Okun, A. (1977) 'Did the 1968 Surcharge Really work?: Comment' *American Economic Review*, March.

Okun, A. (1981) *Prices and Quantities: A Macroeconomic Analysis*, Oxford, Basil Blackwell.

Parkin, Michael and Bade, Robin (1982) *Macroeconomics*, Oxford, Philip Allan.

Pashigian, B. Peter. (1970) 'Rational Expectations and the Cobweb Theory', *Journal of Political Economy*, March/April.

Peacock, Alan and Shaw, G.K. (1976) *The Economic Theory of Fiscal Policy*, 2nd Edition, London, George Allen and Unwin.

Peacock, Alan and Shaw, G.K. (1981) *The Public Sector Borrowing Requirement*, University College at Buckingham, Occasional Papers in Economics No. 1.

Peel, D.A. and Metcalfe, J.S. (1979) 'Divergent Expectations and the Dynamic Stability of Some Simple Macro-Economic Models', *Economic Journal*, December.

Pesaran, M.H. (1982) 'A Critique of the Proposed Tests of the Natural Rate Rational Expectations Hypothesis', *Economic Journal*, September.

Phelps, Edmund S. (1968) 'Money-Wage Dynamics and Labor-market Equilibrium', *Journal of Political Economy*, July/August.

Phelps, Edmund S. (1967) 'Phillips Chrves, Expectations of Inflation and Optimal Unemployment over Time', *Economica*, August.

Phelps, Edmund S. and Taylor, John B. (1977) 'Stabilizing Powers of Monetary Policy under Rational Expectations', *Journal of Political Economy*, February.

Poole, W. (1976) 'Rational Expectations in the Macro Model', *Brookings Papers on Economic Activity*, No. 2, Washington.

Purvis D.D. (1980) 'Monetarism—a Review', *Canadian Journal of Economics*, February.

Santomero, A.M. and Seater, John J. (1978) 'The Inflation-Unemployment Trade-Off: A Critique of the Literature', *Journal of Economic Literature*, June.

Sargent, Thomas J. (1973a) 'Rational Expectations—The Real Rate of Interest and the Natural Rate of Unemployment', *Brookings Papers on Economic Activity*, No. 2, Washington.

Sargent, Thomas J. (1973b) 'Interest Rates and Prices in the Long Run: A Study of the Gibson Paradox', *Journal of Money, Credit and Banking*, February.

Sargent, Thomas, J. and Wallace, Neil (1973) 'Rational Expectations and the Dynamics of Hyperinflation', *International Economic Review*, June.

Sargent, Thomas J. and Wallace, Neil (1975) 'Rational Expectations, the Optimal Monetary Instrument and the Optimal Money Supply Rate', *Journal of Political Economy*, April.

Sargent, Thomas J. and Wallace, Neil (1976) 'Rational Expectations and the Theory of Economic Policy', *Journal of Monetary Economics*, June 1976, reprinted In Lucas and Sargent (eds) (1981).

Shackle, G.L.S. (1939) 'Expectations and Employment', *Economic Journal*, September.

Scheffrin, S. (1983) *Rational Expectations*, Cambridge, Cambridge University Press.

Shiller, Robert J. (1978) 'Rational Expectations and the Dynamic Structure of Macro-Economic Models, A Critical Review', *Journal of Monetary Economics*, January.

Sims, Christopher A. (1982) 'Policy Analysis with Econometric Models', *Brookings Papers on Economic Activity*, No. 1.

Solow, R.M. (1979) 'Alternative Approaches to Macroeconomic Theory: A Partial View', *Canadian Journal of Economics*, August.

Solow, R.M. (1980) 'On Theories of Unemployment', *American Economic Review*, March.

Springer, William (1975) 'Did the 1968 Surcharge Really Work?', *American Economic Review*, September.

Springer, William (1977) 'Did the 1968 Surcharge Really Work? — Reply', *American Economic Review*, March.

Stein, J.L. (ed.) (1976) *Monetarism*, Amsterdam, North Holland.

Stein, J.L. (1982) *Monetarist, Keynesian and New Classical Economics*, Oxford, Basil Blackwell.

Tanzi, Vito (1980) 'Inflationary Expectations, Economic Activity, Taxes and Interest Rates', *American Economic Review*, March.

Taylor, J.B. (1975) 'Monetary Policy during a Transition to Rational Expectations', *Journal of Political Economy*, October.

Taylor, J.B. (1980) 'Aggregate Dynamics and Staggered Contracts', *Journal of Political Economy*, February.

Tobin, James (1977) 'How Dead is Keynes?', *Economic Inquiry*, October.

Tobin, James (1980) 'Are New Classical Models Plausible Enough to Guide Policy?', *Journal of Money, Credit and Banking*, Part 2, November.

Tobin, James and Buiter, Willem (1976) 'Long-Run Effects of Fiscal and Monetary Policy on Aggregate Demand', in Stein, J.L. (ed.) *Monetarism*, Amsterdam, North-Holland.

Turnovsky, S.J. (1980) 'The Choice of Monetary Instruments under Alternative Forms of Price Expectations', *Manchester School*, March.

Weintraub, E. Roy (1977) 'The Microfoundations of Macroeconomics: A Critical Survey', *Journal of Economic Literature*, March.

Weintraub, Robert (1980) 'Comment' in Fischer, Stanley (ed.) *Rational Expectations and Economic Policy* Chicago, University of Chicago Press.

Wilson, T. (1976) 'The Natural Rate of Unemployment', *Scottish Journal of Political Economy*, February.

Wogin, G. (1980) 'Unemployment and Monetary Policy under Rational Expectations: Some Canadian Evidence', *Journal of Monetary Economics*, January.

Index